GURVITCH

EXPLORATIONS IN
INTERPRETATIVE SOCIOLOGY

GENERAL EDITORS

PHILIP RIEFF
Benjamin Franklin Professor of Sociology
University of Pennsylvania

BRYAN R. WILSON
Reader in Sociology, University of Oxford
Fellow of All Souls College

GURVITCH

by

GEORGES BALANDIER

---

translated from the French by
MARGARET A. THOMPSON
with the assistance of
KENNETH A. THOMPSON

BASIL BLACKWELL · OXFORD

ISBN 0 631 15590 2

Library of Congress Catalog Card Number 73-94341

First published in French as
Gurvitch
Copyright © Presses Universitaires de France, 1972,
and translated by arrangement

Text set in Linotype Juliana
Display matter set in Monotype Spectrum
Printed in Great Britain by
Western Printing Services Ltd., Bristol

CONTENTS

A BRIEF BIOGRAPHY

Georges Gurvitch was never an established philosopher: this was by personal choice and because he was closely involved in the great changes of this century. His refusal to settle into a routine existence, to establish a theoretical system and a political allegiance, anticipated the great rebellion of today's youth. He developed a zest for polemics and a disgust of intellectual comforts and compromises, which produced resentments that still linger on. Gurvitch was committed to the battle of ideas, and the dialectic was his weapon; from it he derived a strength—though illness threatened his life—and a certain youthfulness which he retained until he had a heart attack in December 1965.

This man of medium build, ever active, with a penetrating look, commanded respect; and fear, for he was a merciless detector of the mediocre, the lukewarm and the complacent. He liked to unmask people, he *had* to demystify; it was a passion which could drive him to excess or error—and he knew it. His friendship, selective and severe, though with some tenderness, never diminished once it had been acquired. This was a basic characteristic, just as he was also always basically a 'militant protagonist of a revolution which would guarantee human liberty', to use his own words.

Revolution and liberty always remained the focus of his intellectual horizon. A short while before his death, he had undertaken the writing of a sociology of the Bolshevik Revolution; he saw this project as the one which would bring out the full significance of his earlier publications. Born in November 1894 in Noworossisk, he was already a noted young university man when

the Revolution took place. He was a close observer of it for
several years (up to 1920) and a critical participant: he met
Lenin, knew Trotsky, and observed with mistrust the setting-up
of centralized organizations. During this period, however, his
involvement did not hold up a rapid academic career: in 1915 his
first dissertation was published in Dorpat, dealing with the
'political doctrine of Prokopovitch' and his 'sources' (Grotius,
Hobbes, Pufendorf); in 1917 his study of 'Rousseau and the
declaration of rights' appeared. This year was the year of his
agrégation and his first position: he was appointed lecturer at the
University of Leningrad. In 1919 he was appointed professor at
the University of Tomsk.

His 'Russian' career was short: in the year 1920 he left his
country. He dreamed of another revolution which would com-
bine the revolutionary committees with decentralized socialist
planning. From his experience and his contact with philosophers
he began to develop his plans for a sociology which he was to
work on throughout his life. His wife, Dolly, was the privileged
confidante of his criticisms (of revolutionary practice) and this
ambition (regarding the developing social science). Gurvitch was
a man constantly on the move, his intellectual journey not easily
separable from his other journeys. He wanted to be a great ex-
plorer of intellectual territories. As soon as he began his higher
degree studies he sought formative sources not only in Russia,
but also in Germany and central Europe. And he discovered with
excitement the profound transformation in thinking, that Husserlian phenomenology had brought about beyond the Rhine. From
1921 to 1924 he taught in the Russian department of the University of Prague. It was then that he took the step which led him
from metaphysics to experience. He became interested in various
formulations of post-Kantianism; he soon came to know Bergson's
work; but it was Fichte—whose *later* philosophy greatly fascinated him—that left the most lasting impression. Fichte, Husserl
and Scheler were the favourite guides in an exploration which
led to the outlining of 'present-day trends in German philosophy'.

It was through this work, published in France under that title, in 1930, that he performed the function of innovator and had a considerable influence on young philosophers of the time.

Gurvitch established himself in France in 1925, finding there a country that answered his needs, with the result that he developed an often tempestuous partriotism for it. He then worked hard on a survey of juridical, sociological, socialist and syndicalist literature in the French language. He entered into relationships which were to provide new influences: L. Brunschvicg who was to promote open courses at the Sorbonne devoted to German philosophy; L. Lévy-Bruhl who was to influence his research on moral experience; J. Wahl with whom he was to keep up a long acquaintance; M. Mauss whose forcefulness and originality impressed him and who was to lead him towards a 'total' conception of the social phenomenon; M. Halbwachs whom he was to succeed in 1935 at the University of Strasbourg, etc. This date marked the beginning of his French university career, following the defence of his theses in 1932: *L'idée du droit social* and *Le temps présent et l'idée du droit social*, after teaching philosophy at the Collége Sévigné and a brief temporary post in Bordeaux. This period, which ended with the outbreak of war, was a very active one for him. He devoted himself to the philosophy of law, the study of juridical institutions, the relationships between moral theory and the science of morals. He turned towards theoretical sociology with his essay on 'classification of the forms of sociability' (1937) and his *Essais de sociologie* (1938).

After the French defeat, he rejoined the University of Strasbourg that had 'withdrawn' to Clemont-Ferrand. He was threatened and managed to get to the United States, benefiting from an invitation from the New School for Social Research in New York. And in 1941, he contributed to the foundation of the Free School for Higher Studies in New York, the President of which was Henri Focillon. This period, which ended with his return to Strasbourg in 1945, gave him his truly international outlook. It was the opportunity for new involvements, for a practical concern for countries liberated by the allied victory; his *Déclaration des droits sociaux* (1944) was a programme of social and political action for reconstruction—seen as a socialist construction centred on self-management. This period was also one of fertile critical contact with American sociology. P. Sorokin, his 'American' counterpart in exile, whose attachment to his original country had also been lost, was close to him; and he later came to appreciate Sorokin's criticism of 'testomania' and 'quantophrenia'. The American theorists—T. Parsons and R. Merton—provoked his mistrust, then stimulated a polemical zeal which knew no bounds and extended to their disciples and to all proselytes of functionalism and structuralism. With J. L. Moreno, he established a link between 'microsociology' and the developing 'sociometry'; he contributed to the diffusion of sociometry in France, then detached himself from it, emphasizing the ambiguities of Morenian doctrine and practice. These contacts and debates led him to an assessment of sociology (*Twentieth Century Sociology*, published in 1946) and a questioning of the relation of empirical sociology to theory. He took the measure of both and was confirmed in his original idea of contributing to a sociology of knowledge, a sociology of sociologies. He was obsessed by one question: why do these sociologies suffer from an explanatory crisis to which sociologists dangerously accommodate themselves?

The twenty years which followed his return to France saw the maturation of his work, and the consolidation of his university position (he was elected to the Sorbonne in 1949, then to the École pratique des Hautes Études in 1950, where he encouraged the expansion of the social sciences); but he retained his passion for travelling. He was a visiting professor in Latin America (Brazil, Argentina), Japan, Canada, North Africa and the Near-East, in several European countries (Italy, Yugoslavia, Greece) etc. Each time, his militancy—it would be called 'activism' today —was enriched by new circumstances and influences. This was because these countries were the scene of revolutions and counter-revolutions, cultural nationalism, nationalist and anti- imperialist movements. Gurvitch took sides, particularly during the Algerian war: an attack on his Parisian home revealed that his involvement was not considered futile or without consequences. His passion for socialism could not be separated from his passion for sociology; he always saw sociology, particularly its great French tradition, as an emancipatory knowledge and a pedagogy of liberty.

He quickly recognized and fought the increasing power of organizations, bureaucracies, ruling groups and technocrats within modern industrial societies. But he did not for this reason neglect the organization of sociology; he dreamed of giving it weapons suited to the battles that he wanted to fight. In 1946, one year after his return from the United States, he founded the 'Centre d'Études Sociologiques' (with the support of the CNRS) and there developed original research and teaching, encouraged study and discussion sessions—one of which, entitled *Industrialisation and technocracy*, clearly indicated his preoccupations. In this same year he created the *Cahiers internationaux de Sociologie*, published first by the Editions du Seuil, then by the Presses Universitaires de France; a review with an international circulation, whose editorship he entrusted to me some months before his death through a kind of presentiment. It has now passed its fiftieth issue. Along with the *Cahiers*, in which appeared the most important names in contemporary (French and foreign) sociology, he started the 'Bibliothèque de Sociologie contemporaine', access to which he controlled with great critical rigour. This man of freedom became ruthless in his selections when it was a question of producing scientific knowledge. He was just as ruthless in his struggle against the risks of scientific imperialism; faced with the rise of American sociology, he undertook to set up an organization of French-speaking sociologists: with his Belgian friend H. Janne he founded the 'Association internationale des Sociologues de Langue française'. This was no derisory alliance for linguistic protection. It ensured a defence of theoretical, critical sociology, concerned with the free evaluation of *current* positions, in opposition to an empirical sociology that was often mindless and complacently hegemonic. It was open to all who could use French in communicating the results of their scientific activity. Many of the topics reserved for the periodic 'colloquia' reveal an innovatory orientation: Sociology of under-developed countries, Crisis of explanation in sociology, Significance and function of myths in political life and knowledge, 'New States' and nation-building, Sociology of change, etc.

During the whole period from 1950—the year in which he published *La vocation actuelle de la sociologie*, the first expression of his general sociological theory—to 1965, the year of his death, Gurvitch was constantly concerned with fashioning theoretical and methodological instruments for the use of new generations of sociologists. He brought together the team (including some of his opponents) which wrote the *Traité de sociologie*: two volumes published in 1958 and 1960 respectively. He contributed to the critical literature about the founding fathers: Saint-Simon, Proudhon and Marx to whom he drew closer; and Comte and Durkheim who were less important to him than Mauss. His lectures at the Sorbonne became the testing ground for his thoughts and new theoretical positions. He founded the 'Groupe (later to become the "Laboratoire") de Sociologie de la Connaissance' in which R. Bastide, J. Berque, J. Cazeneuve, J. Duvignaud, L. Goldmann, P. H. Maucorps, A. Memmi, etc. collaborated; this research unit, whose brilliance and non-alignment annoyed the supporters of comfortable sociology, survived him and now publishes occasional volumes in the Anthropos series. This was where his high priority research took place, and with which his life came to an end, with the posthumous publication, in 1966, of his work: *Les cadres sociaux de la connaissance*.

One definite conclusion emerged from this long research: sociology must be dialectical and pluralist. Gurvitch stated his position vis-à-vis this requirement in a famous article in the *Cahiers internationaux de Sociologie*: 'Hyper-empirisme dialectique'. In his 'Intinéraire intellectual' (republished by the journal, *L'homme et la société*, 1, 1966), he retraced the path which had led him to this definition which, he said, 'best describes (his) sociological method'. But it was *Dialectique et sociologie* (1962) his most complete work, which constituted the summit of his achievement and offers the fullest and best expression of his theory. It was to the dialectic that he gave pre-eminence in the task of cementing a close alliance between comprehension and explanation; of revealing the scope of determinism and liberty within any society (*Déterminismes sociaux et liberté humaine*, 1955); and of stimulating criticism of social reality and theoretical statements about it. It was in the name of the dialectic that he conducted his fiercest battles, against analytical procedures and the paralysis which was peculiar to them, against nominalism and formalism, against exclusive constructions of the dialectic and history (and particularly structuralism), and against critiques of dialectical reason (during an attempted debate with Sartre). Uncompromising polemics often placed Gurvitch in the counter-current of scientific fashions. He stated with some pride. 'I am therefore "excluded from the horde", by vocation so to speak.' This exclusion contributed to his 'inclusion' in the contemporary historical movement and, consequently, in the stream of the newly developing social sciences.

THE PHILOSOPHY AND
SOCIOLOGY OF GURVITCH

I. THE YOUNG GURVITCH

To some, Gurvitch was a false philosopher; to others, a philosopher who had strayed into the field of sociology. The former reproached him for having chosen the path which led away from metaphysics and came close to empiricism, the latter for having dressed transcendental speculations in sociological clothing. If one accepts such contradictory statements, the ambiguity seems to lie at the very centre of his work. The transition from metaphysics to experience was made, however, as the result of a rigorous project that Gurvitch himself discussed in order to avoid misunderstandings.

1. ITINERARY

From the beginning, he came up against contradictions and aprioris in systems and discovered the necessity of 'comparing them with each other . . . in order to begin developing one's own picture'. He rejected Marxism and Hegelianism almost as soon as he had become acquainted with them. The first because he found an economic determinism in it which denied itself; he wondered what determined an economy, if, in the last instance, the economy was always determining; he questioned the function of the revolutionary activity, if the progress of society and history was so rigorously determined. The second because he saw it as a 'logomachics logonomy' replacing 'reality by arbitrary syntheses, and real history by the alienation of God in the world and his return to himself'. It was here that Gurvitch broke with those who had first stirred him. He was to retun to them later: Hegel, when his knowledge of the *Phénoménologie de l'esprit* had erased the disastrous effect of the *Philosophie du droit*; Marx, when his method led him to the crucial problem of explanation in sociology, and his continuing involvement in the study of class relations.

The discovery of Max Stirner contributed to the overthrowing of these ephemeral 'idols', but it only served to hasten the rapprochement with Kant and the neo-Kantians. Not only because some of the latter tried to reconcile Marx and Kant, but also (and mainly) because the *critical method* promised to expose all types of dogmatism. But this commitment came to be used against itself. Neo-Kantianism was also challenged, for 'its camouflaged Platonic idealism, its rather primitive anti-psychologism and anti-sociologism'. This was the second transition in which the study of Bergson played a similar role to the study of Stirner during the earlier transition, leading Gurvitch to a *realism* that he never had cause to relinquish.

It was in the company of Fichte that Gurvitch travelled furthest, guided by his absolute realism and his way of combining and contrasting intuition and dialectic. He remained faithful in the face of influences—undergone rather than accepted—exercised by the phenomenology of Husserl and Scheler; in fact, he based his criticisms of the latter, and expressed his preference for the non-phenomenological 'realists', by appealing to Fichte's work. After consulting and deciphering Fichte's unpublished texts, he arrived at a favourable assessment of him. On the credit side he put: the acknowledgement of the constant struggle taking place at the very heart of existence (antinomianism); the thesis according to which neither epistemology nor ethics can be constructed without reference to an ontology; the statement that it is impossible to arrive at the 'trans-subjective' or the 'trans-objective' without the combined action of the dialectic and intuition.

On the debit side he put: the transformation of the negative dialectic into a negative theology of the Absolute; the insufficiency of *dualism* in the explanation of perpetual conflicts, of irreducible antinomies—an ontological *pluralism* is required; the slight attention paid to society, cultural works, collective and individual consciousness. Gurvitch's attachment to Fichte, his ethics and his logic, was based on the view that they 'set in motion a great conflict between creation and system'.

This passionate commitment is better understood if one observes that the thought of the young Gurvitch—until about 1930—involved two streams. The first has just been outlined in his itinerary. The second arose from much reflection about the history of social philosophy and sociology; it was strengthened as a result of 'direct experience of the Russian Revolution'; he went in search of 'positions that were both anti-individualist (i.e. affirming the irreducible reality of the social) and anti-statist (i.e. refusing to equate the social "wholes" with one sector and its possible expressions: the State)'. This development was well worked out. He defended Rousseau from the contradictions of which he was accused, but at the same time charged him with failure in his attempt to discover the social reality through the generality of individual reason. His criticism of this mode of reductionism was pursued for a long time, right up to the moment when it was used with renewed vigour to attack contemporary supporters of stucturalism. Saint-Simon was accepted and retained: his social physiology showed society as a reality in motion (society 'in action') and revealed that collective works transcended the individual participants with whom they interacted. He compared Marx with Proudhon, which led him to study the theorists of revolutionary syndicalism and socialism. But it was Proudhon, compared with Comte and his followers, and the founders of French sociology, who increasingly came to occupy the centre of his theoretical system. Significantly, the last book that Gurvitch made sure to publish was devoted to *Proudhon, sa vie, son ouvre* (1965). Proudhon, whom he considered to be the

'Pascal of the social sciences' really fascinated him. Gurvitch agreed with his conception of social reality: an immanent *totality* composed of several *levels* or dimensions, a creation or product of constant collective effort; his theory of antinomies leading to a critical analysis of social life; his anti-statism that laid bare the oppositions between society and state: oppositions between the 'multiple' and the unitary, the spontaneous and the mechanical, change and the static, creation and repetition.

The second stream of Gurvitchian thought led, by way of theses about social law, to a juridical and political sociology, to a generative conception of societies, to a politico-social vision that favoured 'decentralised economic planning', and pluralist democracy. The two streams of thought are obviously not dissociable. They come together to create a general sociological theory. They are combined in the study of moral experience, in the development of a sociology of the mind—the latter term referring to the objectivised and, to some extent, systematised results of human psychic activity—and in a sociology of knowledge. Gurvitch never stopped hoping for—and with increasing vigour—the collaboration of sociology and philosophy freed from their respective imperialisms. 'By mutual and reciprocal observation and criticism, they could and should, while maintaining their complete autonomy, raise basic questions to which only their continual confrontation is capable of responding ...' This need is not simply a reflection or symptom of the current state of knowledge, or the consequence of a particular intellectual itinerary. It is of a more permanent and fundamental nature.

2. LANDMARKS

In describing his development during the last phase of his academic life, Gurvitch saw it as a dialectical, relativistic hyperempiricism. This definition makes it necessary to look into the basis of his conception of experience, determinism and the dialectic.

B

For the first, he clearly indicated his references: 'theories of the integral experience of the immediate'.[1] Here, there was a break with narrow empiricism. Data from experience was not limited to the senses, but perceived even in the framework of the ideal, the spiritual, the logical, and essences inherent in the senses. The subject of experience was no longer a closed consciousness—'a monad without doors or windows'; consciousness was consciousness of something or someone, it was intentional and 'situated'. On this point, Gurvitch used Husserlian phenomenology as a reference point; he rejected 'transcendental reduction'; he considered that experience always appeared in a dual guise: it was both individual and collective.

The originality of the Gurvitchian contribution appeared in his analyses of the 'levels' of experience. It is possible to discern a large number of these depth levels, but the most general contrast is that between the *superficial* and the *profound*. The first is made up of what appears in consciousness as a consequence of numerous elaborations; it is built by and the product of many mediations; it appears both in the form of daily experience and scientific experience. The second level—the depth level—exists prior to any elaboration, in an immediate or spontaneous manner. According to Gurvitch, these two levels are separated by a chasm and the second is the least accessible; he contrasted *experience* or *intuition* (spontaneous experience) with *knowledge* (considered experience), but the former was 'the root which provided nourishment for the latter'; he showed how the various degrees of *actuality* and *potentiality* of consciousness were linked to each of them.

This theory, which is called the theory of 'the integral experience of the immediate', gives priority to data from intuition, to the content of infinitely varied experience. And every experience has validity, for it is integrated into a universe of experiences which *complement* each other. Borrowing a statement from W.

[1] See particularly *L'expérience juridique et la philosophie pluraliste du droit*, Paris, 1935.

James, Gurvitch concluded that truth is arrived at by means of a *radical empiricism*. His sociology, as well as his general philosophy, was constantly guided by this conclusion.

Temporality, causality and determinism, were three terms that Gurvitch obviously could not dissociate. Their simultaneous examination led him to reject the conception of a total, unique and universal determinism; and to justify this rejection by showing what determinism was not. It was not to be confused either with the metaphysical necessity to whose dominant influence Leibniz subscribed (everything is subject to a divinely pre-established harmony), or with the transcendental necessity defined by Kant (eliminating human liberty from the phenomenal world). Neither could it be reduced to logical necessity, for it was dependent on the order of the *real*, nor to mathematical necessity, for mathematics has only an operative character—it is simply the 'mode of expression of those determinist statements which resort to it'.

Consistent with its etymology, the function of determinism is to *determine* by localizing, by 'situating'. It is defined as 'the integration of particular facts into one of the many real frameworks or concrete universes (experienced, known, or constructed), which remains contingent'; by that very fact, it offers an explanation 'as a function of the understanding of the framework'.[2] This definition involves two statements: real frameworks or concrete universes exist; on the other hand, they possess at least a relative stability without which no determination could occur. Here Gurvitch introduced a precision which affected not only his conception of determinism, but also his general theory: coherence is always relative, the product of a *compromise* between coherence and contingency, continuity and discontinuity, quantity and quality. According to the different spheres of reality, it is one or the other of these aspects which predominate; this explains why the relationships between the facts might be of a different nature—causal, functional, probabalist, or belonging to

[2] *Déterminismes sociaux et liberté humaine*, Paris, 1955.

the same group. This rather wide interpretation of determinism leaves room for a certain indetermination: chance is outside determinism, and liberty transcends it.

In Gurvitch's work, radical empiricism and the acknowledgement of a 'conditional' determinism finally emerged as *dialectical empiricism*. This involved seeing the totally dynamic nature of reality, the relatively unstable combinations of aspects through which this is revealed and, by the same token, a denial of separately attributed essences. It was also a critical step, initiated by 'relentless, intransigent ... unbridled dialectic'; and this exactingness was aimed at the eradication of misleading anxieties about thought that were associated with a misplaced consolidation of reality. Gurvitch evoked it in his consideration of the original inspiration for the dialectic: to assure 'the destruction of all acquired concepts, with a view to preventing their mummification, which arises from their incapacity to apprehend totalities in action, and at the same time to take account of a whole and its parts'.[3] On the one hand, the dialectic is (must be) an *anti-dogmatism*, whereas too often it is misrepresented as an 'apology' (from Plotin to Hegel) or a means which determines an end, or it emerges as an eschatology ('universal reconciliation' in Proudhon, freedom from all 'alienations' in Marx). On the other hand, the dialectic is a means; it permits the 'destruction of everything which is opposed, directly or indirectly, to making contact with the vicissitudes of reality'.

At this point, the Gurvitchian interpretations of experience, determinism and the dialectic are closely related: they form a theoretical whole. This theory refers to a *total* conception of experience: whence its description as *hyper-empiricism*. This is as fluid as the reality that it apprehends; and the *dialetic* alone makes it possible to encompass this fluidity, to stimulate the 'constant overthrow of "systems" in favour of the continual in-depth study of problems'. Gurvitch could not be other than a ruthless opponent of system philosophies, and social theories—

---

[3] Article entitled: 'Hyper-empirisme dialectique'.

such as structualism—which bear that stamp. The whole of the latter part of his life was dominated by this struggle.[4]

II. THE SOCIOLOGIST

Gurvitch tried to dissociate the sociologist from the philosopher within himself: 'In becoming more and more of a sociologist and only a sociologist, I tried to detach my statements from doctrinal tendencies and philosophical conceptions, though not always with success ...'[5] He denounced the bad faith which allowed thinking to succumb to the hidden ideological pressures which result from belonging to a particular civilization, class or group. He emphasized the necessity for reaching a deliberate and *unceasing* restatement of the objective description of society; a knowledge which can never be anything other than approximate, as is the 'reality' that it is considering. He continually redefined the vocation of sociology.

1. THE CONTEMPORARY TASKS FOR SOCIOLOGY

The field of study for sociology is the social reality considered at all *levels*, in all its *aspects*, all its *depth levels*; and recognized as not being reducible to any other reality. It can be perceived in various forms: microsocial bonds, groups, social classes and global societies, but the sociological focus must always be that of the 'total social phenomena'. These latter, which are the irreducible elements of any social reality and its expression *par excellence*, are continually in motion. It is through them that the 'We', groups and societies are endowed with dynamism, and are both creative and created, agents and objects of change. They bring

---

[4] For a wider presentation of these theoretical frameworks, refer to: 1) Gurvitch's main work, *Dialectique et Sociologie*; 2) the work of R. Toulemont, *Sociologie et pluralisme dialectique*, Paris, Louvain, 1955, and P. Bosserman, *Dialectical Sociology*, Boston, 1968.   [5] *Itinéraire intellectual.*

together forces of 'structuration' and 'de-structuration' that are constantly at work. They engender *discontinuities* which are the basis of the natural difference between two neighbouring disciplines (so closely related that Durkheim predicted their fusion): sociology and history.

The sociology of the twentieth century must measure its progress in relation to the sociology of the previous century: it is 'existential', multi-dimensional; it is a sociology 'in depth'. This description requires an explanation. In the eyes of the experienced sociologist, the social reality is a precarious arrangement of levels, strata or stages. They interpenetrate and influence each other mutually, from the ecological and morphological foundation right up to 'mental states and collective psychical acts'. Furthermore, they enter into conflict; their relationships are dialectical and in tension. These 'vertical' tensions are in addition to the 'horizontal' conflicts and tensions existing at every level —the antagonisms between social classes provide a good illustration of this. Both are inherent in any social reality; sociology must seek to bring them to the 'surface'. Its *vocation* is to develop its capacity for revealing the contradictions and latent tensions existing in any society, to combat ('in a relentless struggle') the enterprises designed to conceal the bitter drama which takes place on and between the various levels of society. 'Depth' and/or pluralist sociology had philosophical antecedents with Bergson and the phenomenologists, sociological antecedents with Proudhon, Marx and Durkheim who distinguished levels sometimes described as facts of structure, function and representation.

But these forerunners assumed philosophical positions which affected their sociological theories; these theories remained under the influence of prior 'theses', whilst sociology as a science has nothing to do with particular philosophical positions. The obstacle can be removed only if the sociologist has recourse, without concessions, to a *radical empiricism*. This statement raises formidable questions of method.

2. THE SOCIOLOGICAL METHOD ACCORDING TO GURVITCH

It must allow one to avoid both the pitfalls of positivism and the illusions and mystifications of dogmatism. To this end, it must accept a certain number of constraints.

(A) It is *hyper-empiricist*, leaving philosophy its prerogatives, and requiring a categorical rejection of all value judgements. But, notes R. Toulemont in his study on Gurvitch's work, the 'positivity' of sociology is not from positivism, which is, in fact, a ready-made system like all the others. This step requires absolute submission to 'experience'; it considers *all* the data, all the fluctuations of collective experience *and* takes account of the fact that in perceiving them it modifies them. 'What makes experience so close to the dialectic which, in a sense, acts as its driving force, is that it continually breaks its own frames of reference, and is like a veritable Proteus: it escapes us when we think we have it; we are duped by it when we think we have penetrated its secret . . .'[6] Gurvitchian hyper-empiricism requires fidelity to 'experience' at any price.

(B) He wanted to arrive at a global understanding of the social reality, and the concept of *totality* expressed this aim. The sociological method is conducive to the consideration of all the levels at once. Some areas (general sociology, economics, politics) compel one to 'take account of several depth levels'; others (morphology, socio-technology, sociology of cultural works, etc.), focus more particularly on one of these, but nevertheless keep it in its context and *situate* it in the whole.

This methodological characteristic is one logical application of the notion of 'total social phenomenon'. Gurvitch took seriously Mauss' warning in the *Essai sur le don*: 'Having necessarily divided and abstracted rather too much, sociologists should strive to reconstitute the whole'. It is no longer a question of going from the simple to the complex, in a Durkheimian

[6] Cf. 'Hyper-empirisme dialectique'.

perspective, but of reversing the direction of the development in order to explain the apparently simple.

The notion of 'total social phenomenon' refers to both the objective totality of society and the consciousness which embraces this reality. It reveals this consciousness not only in all its complexity (thus compelling the rejection of sectional empiricism), but also in its creativity (compelling a dynamic and generative interpretation). Gurvitch indirectly evoked this interpretation in his presentation of Saint-Simon's 'social physiology': social existence 'is both collective and individual effort; material and spiritual production; action transforming nature, society and its participants; the transcendence of established structures; collective creation ... society produces itself, as well as its participants, its milieux, its tools, its organizations, its regimes, its cultural works'.[7] The sociological method must apprehend the 'social whole' without dispossessing it either of its concrete content or its dynamism which make it a 'creative collective whole'.

(C) Sociological method is distinguished from other totalizing sciences (particularly history) in that it is *typological*. 'It generalises to a certain degree, but with the aim of revealing the specificity of the type. By constructing qualitatively different types, it individualises to a certain degree, but with the aim of discovering the frameworks which might recur.'[8]

The typology defined by Gurvitch is clearly differentiated from the 'ideal' typology developed by Max Weber. It is both qualitative and discontinuous. R. Toulemont rightly emphasized this characteristic: 'The social types are distinguished by the presence in them of elements which, if completely actualised, would end in completely separating them ... It is the distinction on the basis of these elements which makes for the irreducibility of social types.'[9] But one can go further. The number

[7] Cf. C. H. de Saint-Simon, *La physiologie sociale*, Paris, 1965.
[8] Cf. *La vocation actuelle de la sociologie*, Paris, 1950.
[9] *Op. cit.*, chapter V.

and diversity of concrete social phenomena means that the construction of their types and their classification must always refer to several distinctions; they are made on the basis of a pluralism which takes account of the vertical 'dimension' (the 'depth levels') and the horizontal 'dimension' (from microsocial bonds to groups) of the social reality. The type focuses in some way on one aspect of this social reality, or some of the problems that it raises, but it never excludes the aforementioned dual dimensional reference.

(D) This flexibility of development is made specific as soon as one remembers that the sociological method is intrinsically *dialectical*. This governs not only the operational procedures to which it has recourse, but also the relationships that sociology has with other social sciences.

Gurvitch defined five operational procedures, all necessary and to be used either concurrently or jointly:

'Dialectical complementarity' reveals that 'what appears to be a reciprocal exclusion of contrary terms or elements' can be seen 'in the dialectical light as twins, as doublets, in which one is a function of the other and thereby part of the same whole'. The various social types—from those which depend on the microsocial order to those in global societies—are included in a dialectic of complementarity; they appear to enter into conflict with each other, but 'without each other they have no meaning'; they can be neither isolated nor reduced to any one of them.

'Mutual dialectical involvement' leads to 'discovering in the elements or terms that at first sight seem heterogeneous or contrary, certain sectors which are interpenetrated to a certain degree, or are partially immanent in each other'. According to Gurvitch, it is impossible to determine the relationship between psychic life and social life without having recourse to this relationship of involvement; 'for there are psychic elements in the social, and social in the psychic'.

'Dialectical ambiguity' refers to the fact that 'everything that depends on human reality bears the mark of ambiguity and ambivalence'; this state of things requires the application of the dialectical process which 'corresponds' to it. The elements constituting the social 'totalities' are interpenetrated without being destroyed, are linked together while remaining largely irreducible, and enter into a field of attractions and repulsions. And the ambiguity is so much more emphasized when these 'totalities' are in action; the ambivalence can be exacerbated in the 'relationship between the spontaneous (linked to the total social phenomena), the structures and organization'.

'Dialectical polarization' is limited, but not as a special procedure, or the intangible expression of dialectical development (in the Hegelian sense). Only the analysis of a real life problem or *circumstance* makes it sometimes necessary to have recourse to it. In the first case, it is a question of taking it to the extreme: thus, in the study of relationships between determinism and human liberty, one might show that these aspects are not antinomic and might exist only in an intermediary zone (between two extremes or poles). In the second case, it is a question of 'circumstances' where the tensions, ever present in all social life, become real antinomies: for example, in revolutionary situations where the 'spontaneous' provokes the organized superstructures.

Finally, there is the 'reciprocity of perspectives' (a term borrowed from Théodor Litt) which has been raised to the rank of a frequently quoted principle. It allows one 'to discover, in elements admitting neither identification nor separation, a reciprocal immanence that has become so intense that it leads to a parallelism or a relatively close symmetry between their manifestations'. It is particularly necessary in the interpretation of the relationships between the individual and society. The individual and society reveal, at all levels, 'a tendency towards reciprocity of perspectives': for example, the struggle between the different groups in which the individual participates corresponds to 'the struggle between the different "Me's" of the same individual playing various social roles in these groups'.[10]

[10] For development of this point, see *Dialectique et sociologie*, Part 2.

If the dialectic is to contribute to exposing dogmatism, it must itself be de-dogmatized; none of the operational processes that it governs provides the key solution; no profound explanation can be found within its limits alone, although it—and it alone—allows for the understanding of social phenomena in their perpetual dynamism. Before going on to consider sociological explanation, it is necessary to specify in what sense the dialectic affects the relationships between the social sciences. These relationships do not result only from the complexity of social reality, and its action, but also from the position of these sciences with regard to social reality. They can be defined by three statements: the differences between sociology and history on the one hand, and particular social sciences on the other, are based not only on the specificity of methods, but also on the fact that the former are concerned with the perception of *ensembles*, and the second with the perception of *levels* of social reality; the historicity typical of all societies (those which are called 'Promethean' in Gurvitch's restricted interpretation) creates a special relationship between sociology and history; the conceptual dialectic between sociology and the other social sciences reflects, at least partially, the ideological positions of the representatives of these disciplines. Within the framework of these relationships, the dialectic between these sciences (their methods, their concepts, their 'constructions') contributes to freeing each one from dogmatism and to frustrating any claims to scientific imperialism; in the end it forces their actual collaboration.[11]

Gurvitch said of the dialectic: 'It leads us to the threshold of explanation in sociology, but never crosses this threshold.' Elsewhere he stated that all crises in sociology (except those which reflect critical social situations) are linked to the problem of explanation; either because of an attempt to 'explain too much', or the use of false explanations (for example, by describing certain factors as predominant), or because of a reduction of sociology to a naïve or dull sociography.

[11] *Ibid.*, 'La dialectique entre la sociologie et les autres sciences sociales'.

Having defined the position of 'sociological' determinism and shown how its expression varies, Gurvitch proposed certain 'fundamental rules' for explanation in sociology: (1) the predominance of the total in relation to the particular, of the global in relation to the partial—which leads from the abstract to the concrete; (2) the consideration of structures without their being taken as the end of the explanation, for they are 'only a stage in the pursuit of the total social phenomena'; (3) despite the pre-eminence of the global, the obligation to take account of antinomies and conflicts between constituent elements into which these phenomena flow; (4) recognition of the fact that the relationships between levels of social reality vary in their hierarchy, according to the type of society and sometimes even the circumstances; (5) the necessary rapprochment between sociological and historical explanation.

These rules of scientific conduct, though they are necessary, are not sufficient. Their full validity is realized only if one remembers the more general, and in some way preliminary, conditions which govern sociological explanation. There are three: without a general theory (a system of hypotheses subject to verification), explanation is impossible; explanation is unseparable from understanding, for both are merely 'inseparable moments of the same process'; and finally, if the social frameworks escape definition by laws (causal, functional or genetic), sociological explanation can nevertheless have recourse to direct integration in ensembles, to functional correlations and tendential regularities, and above all to singular causality. Such are the means which assist in the continual search for explanation, pointing towards those areas in society which are constantly the sources of its re-creation. Gurvitch wanted to use them in the de-dogmatized study of 'the most striking phenomena of our period': fascism, social revolutions, technocracies, etc.

3. THE SOCIOLOGY OF GROUPS AND CLASSES

It is in this area that Gurvitch best reveals his orientation and the application of his theory; it is here that he makes clear his anti-dogmatic, realist and pluralist demands. The criteria that he uses to define the collective unit, represented by the social group, demonstrate this.

The first of them is the *real* character of this type of unit: the social group is not an 'ensemble' of individuals determined as a function of statistical properties; neither can it be reduced to a simple system of relationships or a collection of social roles; it is not to be confused with the sum of its constituents. It constitutes a particular type of unit which encompasses all of these and imposes a new form on them. However, this unit is only *partial*, for the social group is not isolated: it has to be integrated in a totality which transcends it—the global society. Groups 'are usually directly *observable*' in terms of different sociability relations; they are differentiated in a way that is 'perceptible from outside' by behaviour, symbols and models, material objects, etc.; they have a certain stability. Furthermore the group is a continuous creation, it involves a collective attitude that is both lasting and *active*: 'in order for a group to exist, active sociability must predominate over passive sociability within it'. It is the common work and its continuity which principally determines the group. Lastly, it appears as a '*structurable* social framework' to the extent that, as a real ensemble and system of equilibria, it always constitutes an incipient social structure.

Gurvitch multiplied the criteria necessary for a classification of social groups, and he was criticized for it; the critics overlooked his desire to reject the spirit of systematization in order to apprehend reality in all its complexity and diversity. He retained 15 characteristics which might give rise to a greater number of combinations: number of functions (uni-, multi- and suprafunctional groups); nature of functions and orientation;

number of participants; anticipated duration (according to whether or not causes for dissolution occur); rhythm, including the incidence of replacement of participants; degree of dispersion, from 'distant' groups to permanent groups; mode of formation: actual participation whether voluntary or imposed; mode of access: 'open' groups, 'conditional access' groups, 'closed' groups; degree of organization and principle governing it; relationship with the global society, for certain groups such as ethnic groups, national minorities, universal churches—are unwilling to accept 'penetration' from it; degree of compatibility between groups; mode of constraint, meaning that the group has either an authoritarian or a democratic character; degree of unity according to the mode of synthesis assuring its formation—'unitary', or 'federalist' or 'confederalist' grouping. It is from these characteristics that Gurvitch suggested a definition of social classes; they are 'particular groupings that are real and "distant", characterised by their suprafunctionality, their tendency towards developed structuration, their resistance to penetration by the global society, and their radical incompatibility with each other'.[12] This consolidatory step, which led to a second, long definition, offered as a 'detailed' definition, provoked the accusation of formalism. The attack is unimportant if one bears in mind the fact that Gurvitch undertook to divest the controversy about classes of its ideological content. This shows to what extent he considered the debate decisive for the orientation of sociology and, further, for the orientation of social practice.

He denounced the general usage of the concept of class by explicitly raising the problem of the emergence of social classes, suggesting that 'before the advent of capitalism and industrialisation, it was more a question of *estates, orders, ranks* and *corporations*'. Systems of domination, hierarchy and inequality, which are combined in various degrees of complexity and constitute the framework of every society, do not necessarily create a class society. Furthermore, the existence of 'groups with an

[12] G. Gurvitch, *Etudes sur les classes sociales*, 1966, posthumous edition.

economic affinity'—which determine the 'condition', to use an old term—is not a sufficient basis for a society of this type. One cannot escape from the necessity to provide an adequate definition of this social formation, either by viewing classes as hierarchized social categories 'on the basis of general opinion' (L. Warner's position), or by breaking the unity of the concept so as to distinguish economic and political classes, etc. The task requires a critical evaluation, a historical perspective that considers the earliest discussions of the problem of classes by the founding fathers (Saint-Simon, Proudhon, etc.) and Marx, right up to recent interpretations, which are generally loose and compromising. As Gurvitch observed, one is struck by the fact that the abundance of literature has hardly contributed at all to clarifying the concept of class.

In his *Études sur les classes sociales*, Gurvitch devoted his first section to an examination of the concept in Marx and 'certain Marxists' (Kautsky, Lenin, Bukharin, Lukačs). He concluded this inventory with a criticism of the Marxist conception of classes. He recognized that this was based on an 'important sociological discovery', but one that was insufficiently specified. By placing all the emphasis on the role played in production, by considering only the state and political organizations (parties) as particular groups, Marxist theory fails to recognize the relationship with other groups and limits the field of conflicts (neglecting those which operate within classes and between groups and classes). Similarly, major problems are raised, but not completely resolved: the problem of class consciousness, insoluble in 'the absence of a class psychology'; the problem of the number of classes, despite the assertion of dual polarization —proletariat, bourgeoisie; the problem of the birth of classes, because of the reluctance to tie it solely to the development of capitalism. Finally, Gurvitch reproached the Marxist conception for 'its connection with an eschatological doctrine concerning the role of the proletariat'.

His evaluation of non-Marxist theorists seems even more

disenchanted, even though they contributed to such advances as dissociating the theory of classes from the philosophy of history, pluralizing the role of classes as a function of different structures and social circumstances, and separating the problem of social classes from the *general* problem of the State. The least devastating evaluation concerned Halbwachs' contribution—representative of the Durkheimian school—to the extent that 'he tried to synthesise the sociological, economic and psychological points of view'. At the end of his critical inventory, Gurvitch attempted a contribution to the development of a 'positive concept' of class by considering it in its complexity as a total phenomenon, by integrating it into a general theory of social groups. This definition excluded neither class consciousness, nor the 'cultural works' that classes produce: they are an integral part of their reality, and contribute to their 'structuration'. Furthermore, the 'positive' knowledge of classes is inseparable from the consideration of the role that they play as social frameworks affecting the system of knowledge.

4. SOCIOLOGICAL KNOWLEDGE AND THE SOCIOLOGY OF KNOWLEDGE

It is banal simply to observe that every kind of knowledge has a 'social coefficient'; it is less banal to take the observation seriously and to try, as Gurvitch did, to 'place knowledge in a sociological perspective'. This step soon acquired a critical aspect, in that it denounced the belief in cognitive judgements as possessing universal validity, and challenged the assertion that thought is the prerogative of individual consciousness. The existence of 'collective' knowledge posed new problems for epistemology, without necessarily attributing unilateral influence to the social factors.

Following on from these initial considerations, a definition might be stated thus: the sociology of knowledge is the study of functional correlations which can be established between the kinds, forms and systems of knowledge on the one hand, and the social frameworks—global societies, social classes, groups and microsocial relationships—on the other. The area can be defined in this way, but the tasks that it sets seem numerous and formidable. In the first stage, the 'varieties' of knowledge must be determined, since sociologists have generally considered only a small number; and then an actual cognitive typology must be developed. Gurvitch described this step as 'a precise and detailed analysis of the *types of knowledge* and their inter-relationship with the *forms of knowledge*'. He divided the first into seven categories, according to their distinctive character-istics:

(A) 'Perceptual knowledge of the external world'. This is where the contributions of external and internal senses pre-dominate, accompanied by implicit or explicit judgements con-firming the reality of what is perceived. It relates to a 'coherent ensemble of images, placed in concrete, specific space and time'. It provides very disparate possibilities for conceptualisation.

(B) Knowledge of external aspects of social reality. The micro-social relationships, groups, classes and societies are then 'per-ceived in their reality and confirmed as veridical by conscious judgement'. This type, which provides knowledge about men, individual and collective human agents, parallel to that about things, is to a high degree a constituent element of the social reality itself.

(C) 'Common sense' knowledge or knowledge 'of everyday life'. It combines the preceding types with knowledge of tech-niques and conventions. It favours traditions, and customs justi-fied by common sense; being essentially practical it helps towards 'orientation in the world and particularly in the *social world*'.

(D) 'Technical knowledge', which is irreducible to any other. It cannot be reduced either to the means used to attain ideal goals (according to the spiritualist view), or to a transmissible applied science (according to the interpretation of crude positivism). It is the result of the wish to 'dominate' the world, to control and

c

manipulate it. It is a constituent part of *praxis*, in the Marxist sense, and is directly integrated in the productive forces. It is therefore 'knowledge which is also action'.

(E) 'Political knowledge'. This is manifested in doctrines, whose relative importance lies less in their intrinsic truth than in the strength of the collective beliefs that they translate. It is expressed not only in texts, speeches and debates, but also in political action and the reactions of public opinion. This is the most 'committed' knowledge; it is 'penetrated' by ideologies, utopias, myths (in the Sorelian sense) and symbols calling for action. It involves 'the clear consciousness of difficulties to be overcome and an acute sense of the behaviour to be adopted in any particular social circumstance'; this requires a new, indissoluble fusion of several kinds of knowledge. Such knowledge was the object of Marx's consideration in his interpretations of ideologies, and of Mannheim in his attempt to construct a sociology of knowledge.

(F) 'Scientific knowledge'. This is constituted from essentially *constructed* operational frameworks and combines the conceptual and the empirical; it is rational. In contrast to political knowledge, it is the least partisan of all. Despite its claims to be detached from social frameworks, it is only relatively independent; and the 'great mistake of positivism' was to ignore the social coefficients which inevitably affect it.

(G) Finally, 'philosophical knowledge'. This exists at the second level, in the sense that 'it is grafted on later to other already established knowledge and it strives to integrate partial manifestations of it into infinite totalities, in order to justify them'. One could say that in this case it is a question of knowledge of knowledge. It is formed at a distance, which compels Gurvitch to say that it is 'esoteric, aristocratic'. It makes individual knowledge predominate over collective knowledge, and though disinterested (or postulated as such), it does involve an element of partisan knowledge which makes it less rational than scientific knowledge.

The second stage consists of relating this cognitive typology to the manifestations of sociability (microsociology of knowledge) and to groups which provide 'frameworks' for knowledge, along with social classes, and global societies. The ultimate goal, for it permits the validation of all the preceding stages, is the study of relationships between systems of knowledge and global social structures. For each type of global social structure the procedure which Gurvitch adopts is the same: to establish the relative strengths, the hierarchy, of the various kinds of knowledge. One single example is sufficient to illustrate this—that of societies corresponding to 'organised, directed capitalism'. This type is defined by five characteristics, namely: (a) The state on the one hand, and trusts and cartels on the other, predominate over all other groupings; (b) the organized apparatus for domination (depending on automation, electronic means, and the *media*) and economic planning occupy the highest position in the depth levels; (c) the development of automation restrains the technical division of labour and consequently, the social division of labour; (d) 'technocratisation' extends into the field of 'human relations' (in the American sense of the term) which is based on manipulation; (e) from the micro-social point of view, passive masses predominate to the detriment of 'communities'. This social formula is particularly vulnerable, for it does not allow for 'the control of the explosive forces' to which it gives rise.

A clearly differentiated cognitive system is associated with this type of society. In first place is 'technical knowledge'; it appears at all levels, and to such a degree 'that all other manifestations of knowledge are influenced by it'; it is the product of a 'dominating omnipresence of techniques'. 'Political knowledge' occupies second place, but it is subject to the influence of technical knowledge both in its doctrines and party programmes, as well as in its spontaneous political forms. It engenders a blind power, lacking discernment in the face of the threats 'which unbridled techniques offer to any social structure'. The 'perceptual knowledge of the external world' and 'common sense knowledge' are also marked by technicization; the former by the *media* and new relationships to space; the latter by instruments and their manipulation, and industrial products. Finally, 'philosophical knowledge', relegated to a lower level, also seems open to the same influences; symbolic logic and positive axiomatics tend to repress other philosophical orientations to such a point that the 'existentialist' reaction could emerge only as a lost cause. Only the 'knowledge of the other and We' resists penetration by technical knowledge; it is nevertheless relegated to the last place and uses all the forms which enable it to maintain itself.

This analysis presented by way of an example, shows how Gurvitch attempted to link dialectically the social frameworks with the modes of production of knowledge and with the forms of 'social control'. They maintain relationships of 'inexhaustible richness', and are ever changing, not only because of the type of society, but also because of circumstances and historical periods. The search for functional correlations through the various types of social formations, historical and current, led Gurvitch to think about the 'present' and to warn against the dangers contained in it.[13]

III. THE THEORETICIAN OF PRAXIS

The dominant preoccupations of Gurvitch were not only theorectical. He wanted sociology to be a *vocation* (rather than the opportunity for an 'occupation') and he always showed—as J. Duvignaud recalled[14]— a certain mistrust of 'sociological

[13] The Gurvitchian concept of the sociology of knowledge has its most complete statement in the posthumous work *Les cadres sociaux de la connaissance*, Paris, 1966. (English translation by Margaret A. Thompson and Kenneth A. Thompson, *The Social Frameworks of Knowledge*, Oxford, Basil Blackwell, 1971.)

[14] J. Duvignaud, *Georges Gurvitch, symbolisme social et sociologie dynamique*, Paris, 1969.

bureaucracy'. He considered that the sociologist's work might assist in the constitution of the social system, because it revealed its deeper reality and went along with its movement. By having the social as the object of investigation, sociology necessarily contributes to its formation.

1. A SOCIOLOGY OF LIBERTY

The being and becoming of social reality involves *human liberty* as a decisive element. This is neither pure contingency nor pure creation *ex nihilo*; it involves a relationship between events, a contribution to their occurrence and an action which is not absolutely discontinuous. It is not the liberty of 'indifference', for humanity would then be given over to the whims of chance and incapable of creating civilizations. It cannot be reduced to the liberty of 'expectation', individual and/or collective, and neither can it be equated with action subject to the sole influence of rational motives.

This negative definition leads to a positive conception. Liberty is an inalienable attribute of human existence; it cannot be deduced or extracted from 'any particular construction', it underlies all work, action, behaviour and realization—and one perceives it through experience; it is the capacity for modification, for transcendence of the determinism which confronts man as an individual and/or member of a society. Manifestations of liberty are clearly distinguished from determined phenomena: by the relative emphasis on contingency, discontinuity, and the qualitative; by the contrast between the 'completed' (which refers to the irreversible past) and the 'process of happening' (which refers to the present and projects into the future); by the intervention of the 'clairvoyant' will, a volitional intuition.

Human liberty which is experienced collectively as well as individually, is therefore doubly defined; it is voluntary, innovatory, creative action; it is 'forced to clear away, overthrow, and break down all obstacles and to modify, transcend, recreate all situations'. This liberty attempts not only to modify obstacles external to the action, but also 'to modify its own agents'; it annuls the classical opposition between the contingent and the possible—to the extent that it can open up possibilities 'by modifying and reversing situations, by setting up new circumstances, by creating new frames of reference, and through those means, by provoking the appearance of new contingencies'. Thus conceived, liberty reveals society in its aspect of continuous creation; it relates to the plans and active will of different social actors.

Gurvitch specified that the degrees of human liberty stretch to infinity, but nevertheless, he retained six main stages:

(A) 'Liberty of subjective preferences'; here the driving force predominates over the motive, and contingency is strongly emphasized; this is a 'lazy liberty'.

(B) 'Innovatory liberty'; which involves a stronger, more enlightened will than that used in choices made according to preferences, a will tending towards the concrete application of rules, directives, rational plans; this is a 'moderate ... patient ... careful liberty'.

(C) 'Liberty of choice': a stage 'where the clairvoyant will which guides the act is translated into actuality for the first time'; it breaks open closed social universes, by going beyond the alternatives; it rests on a choice which acknowledges its direction 'and consequently its motives and driving forces', in the actual course of action.

(D) 'Inventive liberty' allows for the avoidance of alternatives that are too 'threatening' by bringing up new possibilities for the consideration of the will; it supposes collaboration and competition between intellectual imagination and the intuition of the will; but it remains a 'strategic' or 'manoeuvering' liberty—it is therefore, in this sense, the liberty that man uses as a political being.

(E) 'Decision-making liberty' leads to the elimination of obstacles: it does not skirt them, but confronts them directly and avoids using trickery; it is often anticipatory; it is a 'risky' or 'heroic liberty' since the collective and individual agents have to 'play all to win all'; it therefore runs the risk of creating the irreversible as a result of over-precipitate choices.

(F) 'Creative liberty' is the culminating point of human liberty, for it approaches demiurgic man. It is continually creating and recreating and, in this movement, is supported by all the other degrees of liberty; it contributes most to the work of constructing social reality. It is the liberty *par excellence* that is never completely achieved and 'cannot find in itself the transcendence of its drama'.[15]

Gurvitchian sociology is a sociology of liberty, but it is never transformed into an apology for a sociology of liberty or into a libertarian ideology. Gurvitch clearly stated that liberty is ambiguous; it can destroy as well as construct, and can lead towards either negative or positive values; it can be destroyed in the confrontation between collective and individual liberties. The reminder is frequent and serious: liberty is not an absolute; it is *situated*, and framed by reality, it is conditional and relative. It is only relatively determined, placed between contingency and necessity, discontinuity and continuity. In this sense even the most enterprising, the most creative or the most revolutionary liberty could never completely erase continuity.

2. AN ANTI-TECHNOCRATIC ALTERNATIVE

At a sociological conference held in Paris in 1948, Gurvitch started his fight against the theoreticians of techno-bureaucracy. The principal target was at that time J. Burnham and his *Managerial Revolution*. The main theses of this author are well known: capitalism cannot disappear→socialism does not generally have the capacity to succeed it→the subsequent régime will be defined and controlled by the class of 'managers'. The devel-

[15] See 'Les degrés de la liberté humaine', in *Cah. Int. de Socio.*, XI, 1951 and *Détérminismes sociaux et liberté humaine*, Paris, 1955.

opment of industry and advanced techniques would favour the seizing of economic and political power by a 'directorial class'; and the supremacy of the organized apparatus ensures the 'planning' of the economy and its 'domination' at various levels.

Where Burnham saw an ineluctable evolution, Gurvitch recognized a movement, fatal to all forms of democracy, that he felt had to be strongly opposed: there is no such thing as historical fatality, only mortal 'sociological fatalism'. He started with the observation that techno-bureaucracy occurred 'under the most varied of régimes'. Organized, directed capitalism is one of them: 'The economy is no longer left to free competition, but planned both by the state itself—in the interest of the reigning industrial and financial upper bourgeoisie—and by private trusts and cartels... And furthermore, with the support of the state, which places its vast administrative and bureaucratic machinery at their service.' Centralized collectivist statism is another of these régimes. In the USSR, under Stalin's government, 'the industrial, administrative, military and planning techno-bureaucracy became very powerful'; 'the organs of economic planning which developed the plans and supervised their execution were very important, but neither the workers, nor the peasants, nor the great mass of consumers were directly represented in them'. These two cases, particularly the second, are fraught with ambiguity: therefore they have not eliminated the virtualities of industrial democracy. By contrast, everything is quite clear in the case of fascist and nazi régimes, societies corresponding to the 'fascist techno-bureaucratic' type. This is defined as 'a complete fusion of the totalitarian state with the organisms of economic planning and the organisation of the army, managed by technocratic groups'; groups which originate in the army itself, high administrative personnel, trusts, cartels and banks, etc. The consequence is 'the enslavement of all social classes and all groupings, inasmuch as they exist, to the State, which is itself dominated by cliques, of either techno-bureaucrats, military men or "national liberators" '.

The problem has deep roots. Technocratic ideas are conveyed through a whole current of economic sociology starting with Saint-Simon, who wished to commit the real responsibility for government to the 'industrialists'. Today, the danger from technocracy is increasingly threatening: 'Discretionary powers, linked to the control of powerful technical forces . . . give formidable power to the developing class of technocrats that only complacent sociological optimism could neglect.' However, the means of opposing the establishment of a successful technocracy do exist. Gurvitch lists them, in addition to the suggestion to utilize the divisions and differences of interest between the technocrats against themselves: decentralization of public power and strengthening of the control exercised by its citizens, limitations of the power (both of the State and the technicians) by an autonomous organization of economic planning controlled directly by producers and consumers; effective control of enterprises by producers and consumers. This is the outline of a plan for decentralized, therefore pluralist, collectivism initiated by Proudhon.[16]

3. A CONCEPTION OF SOCIALIST AND PLURALIST DEMOCRACY

In his work devoted to the philosophy and history of law, and his studies defining 'future democracy' and socialism, Gurvitch gradually worked out his social plan. He was opposed to individualism and statism, which *both* lead to the rule of force and repressive powers. He revealed himself with increasing passion and consistency as a democrat and a collectivist. According to him, democratic principles are in agreement with the philosophical option of 'transpersonalism'; the sovereignty of the people is the sovereignty of a concrete whole in which all the members are jointly responsible, and equality becomes a 'function

[16] Refer to the book edited by G. Gurvitch, *Industrialisation et technocratie*, Paris, 1949, and its development in *Les Cadres sociaux de la connaissance*, Paris, 1966.

of the whole', through equivalence of personalities. These principles can be realized in any democratic organization, not only in the State, and they are the *only ones* allowing society to be based on law. In *L'Expérience juridique*, published in 1935, the statement is clearly formulated: 'Democracy is the necessary, the only possible way towards the realisation of law within a social organisation . . . A non-democratic power is a power instituted above and beyond the law.' This leads to the recognition of the sovereignty of *social law*, whose organization is ensured by democracy. But how can social law be defined? Gurvitch always considered it in his various works as something for the benefit of the 'common interest'—an ensemble of balances between different particular and often opposing interests, operating for the benefit of the 'whole'. Social law has as its *function* the management of the common life of the members of a totality; as the *basis* of its necessary force the fact that it is created directly by the totality in which it is integrated; and as its *structure*, that which ensures the direct participation of the totality in its functioning.

The Gurvitchian conception of socialism is not differentiated from his idea of democracy: the first is the economic aspect of the second and the condition which allows it to develop all its potentialities. More precisely, socialism is 'a system of rational organisation of the economy which is aimed at the suppression of the power of man over man, to the extent that this power depends on property relationships'. It does not deny property but seeks to prevent power over things being converted into power over men. The only radical solution is to extend *federalist property* to the whole of economic society so that the rights of all of its members are kept in balance. It is therefore a collectivism which rejects unrestricted appropriation by the state or by the 'society' of the means of production and the means of ensuring control of the economic process.

The *Déclaration des droits sociaux* (1944) takes up and develops this theoretical position, makes clear the normative intention, and presents itself as a suggested plan for the attention of the constituents who would have the responsibility for reconstruction after the French defeat. This is the point where Gurvitch expresses most clearly his wish to intervene in the course of events, to convert his sociology into historically decisive practice. The work reaffirms his adherence to *pluralism*. This is fundamental: the texture of social life is 'characterised by a fundamental pluralism *de fait*, the tension between groups and their changing equilibria constituting the fundamental social material'; it is also —and in contrast—an ideal: it consists of 'a harmony between variety and unity, reciprocally producing an equilibrium between personal values and values of groups and ensembles, a reciprocal immanence between the whole and the many parts.

This pluralist view leads to the definition of a plurality of rights (rights of man, citizen, producer and consumer) restricting power, and the proclamation of the right of individuals, groups and their ensembles in 'a pluralist organisation of society that is capable of guaranteeing human liberty in current conditions'. This organization involves many restrictions, particularly the many controls on participants. It must restrain the power of the State, not for the purpose of neutralizing it, but in order to strengthen it in its appropriate domain; likewise, the functions withdrawn from the State are mainly transferred to a national economic organization. The constant concern is to organize 'the negation of exploitation, domination, despotism, inequality and unjustified limitation of the freedom of individuals and groups, wherever it concerns integration and participation in ensembles'. It was therefore a total—and anti-totalitarian—reconstruction of society which was contemplated and outlined.

In some ways, the Gurvitchian plan aimed at the impossible, to bring about the impossible from the rubble left by the war. The emphasis was on the means to a real economic democracy. Property is legitimized only because of its social function, and its individual form is limited or contained by the 'public collective' and particularly the 'social collective' forms—corresponding to federative ownership as

defined by Proudhon. The consumer is drawn out of his passivity
and asssociated with the general management of the economy.
The producer, who is guaranteed the right to work—whose re-
muneration is the result of 'collective agreements'—is recognized
as having the right to participate in the management and control
of the enterprise ('councils of control and management') and the
general economy ('economic councils').[17]

This project is only fully meaningful if one remembers Gurvitch's profound attachment to Proudhon's intellectual heritage,
considered to be 'much more revolutionary' in many aspects
than Marx's. He found in it: (a) a bold, virulent criticism of the
social order; (b) an early discussion of a scientific socialism; (c) a
plan for future society seen as 'positive anarchy' and 'industrial
democracy'; (d) a definition of the means of realizing this, of
provoking the proletarian revolution. He agreed with Proudhon's forecast that decentralized, pluralist collectivism would
replace organized capitalism. It would be a collectivism that
would depend on worker self-management and would establish an
equilibrium between a federalized ownership of the means of
production (controlled by the industrial democracy of workers)
and an economic democracy with limited functions. In a brief
but remarkable presentation of Proudhon's work and action,
Gurvitch paid highest tribute to him by saying: 'A hundred
years after his death, the contemporaneity of Proudhon compels
recognition as much in the East as in the West.' And he used to
call himself, with mocking false-modesty, 'a failed Proudhonian'.

His model reinforced his rejection of received positions and
knowledge, hinderances to creative freedom, compromises made
in the name of realism. J. Duvignaud described Gurvitchian sociology as having 'subversive' vigour. This is certainly so, through
its content and the social plan which it proposed. Gurvitch contrasted 'depth' sociology with the flat interpretations of social
reality, the total social phenomenon with the arbitrary slices of
the latter, the generative conception of society with static non-

[17] La déclaration des droits sociaux, New York, 1944 and Paris, 1946.

problematical interpretations, sociological realism with barely concealed nominalisms, and critical sociology with complacent or imperious sociologies. He was the indefatigable critic of a certain deluded, unthinking empiricism, lending suport to P. Sorokin's charge against 'quantophrenia', 'testomania' and 'testocracy'. He wanted to be the agent provocateur of a 'sane reaction' against formulae and techniques 'which lead nowhere except to the mania for the serious proffering of tautologies, and for the elimination of all explanation through an often falsified "sociography". In this area, he went to extremes, doubtless because he wanted to reduce as rapidly as possible a danger that he considered fatal. A sociology that is not closely associated with theory and empirical research *and* in 'close collaboration' with philosophy and history, Gurvitch felt must rapidly become an insignificant sociology.

Gurvitch, who described himself as a researcher working 'against the current', was attacked by those who lazily chose to follow the current. They denounced him for the difficulties in his scientific language; laughed at him for the multiplicity of his criteria and the complication of his typologies; challenged him as to the possibility of translating his theory into rules of empirical research, and as to his use of the 'material' underlying his generalizations; emphasized the unfinished nature of some of his theoretical developments. Nevertheless, recent evaluations do him more justice. P. Bosserman in a sympathetic but not uncritical analysis, demonstrated the many contributions of Gurvitch to the innovatory enterprises of contemporary sociology.[18] Before him, P. Sorokin had said that 'G. Gurvitch's contribution both to general sociology and its various branches is one of the most important of our time'.[19] But Gurvitchian sociology gains its most spectacular verification from current events at a time when great social transformations are taking place.

[18] P. Bosserman, *Dialectical Sociology, an analysis of the sociology of G. Gurvitch*, Boston, 1968.

[19] P. Sorokin, *Sociological Theories of Today*, New York, 1966; Chap. 14, 'Gurvitch's empirico-realist dialectical sociology'.

THE WORKS OF GURVITCH

MAJOR WORKS

La doctrine politique de Th. Prokopovitch et ses sources euro-péennes (Grotius, Hobbes, Pufendorf), Dorpat, 1915. In Russian.

Rousseau et la déclaration des droits. L'idée de droits inaliénables de l'individu dans la doctrine politique de Rousseau, Petrograd, 1917. In Russian.

La philosophie du droit de Otto. V. Gierke, Tübingen, 1922. In German.

Introduction à la théorie du droit international, Prague, 1923. In Russian.

L'éthique concrète de Fichte, Tübingen, 1924. In German.

Les tendences actuelles de la pholosophie allemande, E. Husserl, M. Scheler, E. Lask, M. Heidegger, Paris, Vrin, 1st edn., 1930, 2nd edn., 1949.

L'idée du droit social, Paris, Sirey, 1932.

Le temps présent et l'idée du droit social, Paris, Vrin, 1932.

L'expérience juridique et la philosophie pluraliste du droit, Paris, A. Pedone, 1935.

Morale théorique et science des moeurs, Paris, 1st edn., 1937, 3rd edn. rewritten, Presses Universitaires de France, 1961.

Essais de sociologie, Paris, 1938.

Eléments de sociologie juridique, Paris, Aubier, 1940.

Sociology of Law, New York and London, 1942.

La déclaration des droits sociaux, New York, 1944 and Paris, Vrin, 1946.

La vocation actuelle de la sociologie, Paris, Presses Universitaires de France, 1st edn., 1950, 4th edn., 1969.

Déterminismes sociaux et liberté humaine, Paris, Presses Universitaires de France, 1st edn., 1955, 2nd edn., 1963.

Dialectique et sociologie, Paris, Flammarion, 1962.

Proudhon, sa vie, son oeuvre, Paris, Presses Universitaires de France, 1965.

C.H. de Saint-Simon, La physiologie sociale, Paris, Presses Universitaires de France, 1965.

Les cadres sociaux de la connaissance, Paris, Presses Universitaires de France, 1966. Posthumous publication. English translation by M. A. and K. A. Thompson, Oxford, Basil Blackwell, 1971.

Études sur les classes sociales, Paris, Denoël-Gonthier, 1966. Posthumous publication.

WORKS EDITED BY GURVITCH

La sociologie au vingtième siècle (in collaboration with W. E. Moore), 2 vols. Paris, Presses Universitaires de France, 1947.

Industrialisation et technocratie, Paris, A. Colin, 1949.

Traité de sociologie, 2 vols., Paris, Presses Universitaires de France, 1st edn., 1957 and 1960, 3rd edn., 1968.

MAJOR ARTICLES

'La sociologie du jeune Marx', in *Cah. intern de Socio.*, IV, 1948.

'Microsociology and sociometry', in *Sociometry*, XII, 1–3, 1949.

'Hyper-empirisme dialectique', in *Cah. intern. de Socio.*, XV, 1953.

'Le concept de structure sociale', in *Cah. intern. de Socio.*, XIX, 1955.

'La crise d l'explication en sociologie', in *Cah. intern. de Socio.*, XXI, 1956.

'Continuité et discontinuité en histoire et sociologie', in *Annales*, I, 1957.

'Structures sociales et multiplicité de temps', in *Bull. de la Société franç. de Phil.*, 52nd year, 1959.

'Philosophie et sociologie', in *Encyclopédie francaise*, XIX, 1957.

'Dialectique et sociologie selon Jean-Paul Sartre', in *Cah. intern. de Socio.*, XXXI, 1961.

EXTRACTS

I. MY INTELLECTUAL ITINERARY

The first two years of my graduate studies (1912–1914) which I spent in Russia in the winter and Germany in the summer, were devoted to the study of law and reading the most important political theorists. During this time my thoughts were centred on the various tendencies of neo-Kantian philosophy: Cohen, Natorp, Cassirer, Rickert, Windelband, Volkelt, Renouvier, Hamelin ... In the end I reacted very strongly against every kind of neo-Kantianism, its camouflaged Platonic idealism, its rather primitive anti-psychologism and anti-sociologism. Since neither the discussion between Tarde and Durkheim, nor the sociological formalism of Simmel gave me much satisfaction, I turned to Wilhelm Wundt. In order to better understand his *Völker Psychologies* (*Psychology of Peoples*), he recommended that I study experimental psychology in his laboratory. The only benefit derived from these studies, brief as they were, was to teach me experimentally that direct 'psychophysiological parallelism' was impossible and to show me the absence of a correspondence between time that is experienced, time that is conceptualized and, particularly, time that is measured, and time that is quantified. All these various times have to be distinguished from each other.

At this point, I began to read and study Henri Bergson. *Les donnees immédiates de la conscience* provided the emancipation that I had expected from Wundt's experimental psychology, while *Matière et mémoire* and *L'évolution créatrice,* by liberating me from the influence that Kantian and neo-Kantian idealism

D

still had over me, led me towards a realism that was free from necessitarianism. And yet I was disturbed, and my youthful enthusiasm was somewhat cooled, by the spiritualist emphasis of Bergsonian realism in *L'évolution creatrice*, and its latent individualism, which separated the 'profound me' from the 'superficial me', which alone participated in real social life. In the months that preceded the First World War, I attended the lectures in Heidelberg of Emil Lask who, by using a vigorous dialectic borrowed from Fichte, sought to go beyond idealism within the neo-Kantian framework. In addition to my interests in Fichte, I am indebted to Lask for introducing me to the sociology of Max Weber. At that time, his sociology was seen mainly as a justified reaction to the thought of Rickert, who reduced all scientific method either to generalization or individualization, neglecting the typological method that was appropriate to sociology based on understanding (*Verstehen*).

I was then completing a dissertation in Russian for a university examination on 'La doctrine politique de Théophan Prokopovitch et ses sources européennes: Grotius, Hobbes et Pufendorff'. The gold medal which I was awarded in 1915 was the deciding factor in my academic career. For, having returned to Russia before the commencement of hostilities, and having obtained my master's degree (1917), I enrolled at the University of Petrograd in order to prepare myself for the professoriate which first involved obtaining the *agrégation* for higher education.

During my university years, from 1915 to 1920, i.e. to the time when I received my agrégation and was given responsibility for a course at the University of Leningrad–Petrograd (which I left some months later to emigrate first to Czechoslovakia, then, from 1925, to France, where I acquired French nationality in 1929), my thinking was marked by several turning points, evidence of which can be found in most of my writings:

(A) My interest in realism (which occupies an important place in my present thinking) had, for a short time, brought me close to the 'intuitionism' of two Russian philosophers: Lossky and Frank, and through them, to certain slavophilic ideas related to Greek orthodox religious philosophy. But the danger of mysticism led me back to a dialectical criticism which caused me to distinguish between what is *perceived* through intuition and what is *known* (presupposing a judgement); it also led to an appreciation of the pluralism of reality, that is opposed to any monistic reduction of the multiple to the One. I thus found an absolute realism in Fichte's later works where he arrived at the problem of 'facticity' (Fakizität), through a continual competition and collaboration between intuition and dialectic.

(B) My studies in the history of social philosophy and sociology concentrated mainly on all the various positions that were both anti-individualist (i.e. that affirmed the irreducible reality of the social) and anti-statist (i.e. that refused to equate the social 'wholes' with one sector or one possible expression: the state). I searched for this broader concept of the social in Saint-Simon, Proudhon, Grotius, Leibniz, Fichte and Krause, and even much further back, in Aristotle. I recorded the results of this research much later on in the main thesis of my doctorate: *L'idée du droit social* (1932), to which I shall return later.

Meanwhile I was puzzled by the enigmatic position of Jean-Jacques Rousseau—to some he was an extreme statist, to others an anarchist; to some an individualist, to others he was thought to be placing a value on the reality of social existence. I was intrigued by his concept of 'general will' which is contrasted not only to 'the will of the majority' but also to 'the will of all people' and found to be identical in each individual, inasmuch as the individual and the society are reborn into a new life through the 'social contract'. Furthermore I saw in Kant's categorical imperative nothing more than a weak reproduction of Rousseau's social philosophy. In my book *Rousseau et la déclaration des droits* (1917), while defending Rousseau from the contradictions which he was accused of, and trying to bring out the profundity of his dialectic, I was forced to show the failure of his endeavour:

he hoped to discover social reality by means of the generality of individual reason.

Although Proudhon's criticisms of Rousseau did not always seem to me to be sufficiently thorough, it was he who held the greatest attraction for me, because of his positive doctrine. His notion that what is social can not, without being alienated, be projected outside the participants either as a superior subject or an exterior object; his deep-seated notion of social pluralism seeking to keep the many groups in equilibrium; his negative dialectic; his demonstration of the relativity of all social prediction; his theory of human creation gaining ground over predetermined progress—all this gave me great pleasure. If I could be called Proudhonian, it was particularly so at the beginning of my scientific career. Through Proudhon, I was led to study all the French theoreticians of revolutionary syndicalism, including Sorel, with whom, however, I never felt a great affinity. From the point of view of social theory, I was very much of a Proudhonian and syndicalist at the time of the two Russian revolutions in February and November 1917 (some ten years behind France). This combined rather well with the emergence of 'factory councils' and their tendency to elect representatives not only to the 'central councils' which had political jurisdiction, but also to 'controlling councils' in various companies. British guild socialism which was at its peak after the First World War also had a considerable effect on me.

(C) To all of this was added direct experience of the Russian revolution. By observing, by living through the different reactions of the various milieux, groups and classes, syndicates, cells, councils, new and old organizations, by witnessing the almost total explosion of the old global social structure, I discovered several ideas which later guided me in my sociological work:

(1) Social law develops spontaneously, completely independently of the state and its legal order, and can enter into various relationships with state law.

(2) The depth levels of the social reality, whose hierarchies and relationships can be turned upside down, sometimes contradict each other and at other times interpenetrate.

(3) The group is considered as a microcosm of the forms of sociability.

(4) The global society and social classes are considered as macrocosms of groups.

(5) The possibility of non-statist collectivist planning, based on a pluralist economic democracy and federalist ownership. I recall very well a memorable walk with my wife on the banks of the Karpovka River in Leningrad in 1920, when for a whole spring evening, a few months before we left Russia, I told her all about the sociological theories which I intended to elaborate, the main points of my theses on social law, and my ideas on decentralized collectivist planning.

Since my relativism and realism in sociology were developed to an extreme, *dialectical hyperempiricism*[1] best describes my sociological method. One gets an idea of this method from the complementarities, the mutual involvements, ambiguities, polarizations and reciprocities of perspectives between the microsociological types, types of groups and social classes, and types of global societies; between the depth levels of social reality, whose hierarchy varies with each type of partial or global structure; between the total social phenomena, astructural elements, structures and organizations; between general sociology and particular branches of sociology; between sociology, history and ethnology. The ultimate goal of this method is to arrive at an explanation in sociology, an explanation which, when it becomes causal, is linked to historical explanation. One of the secrets of the junction between theory and empirical research is sociology, along with experimentation as such and the constant renewal of working hypotheses, lies in the very precious material which history provides for sociology. Moreover, history itself

[1] Cf. my study of the same title in the XVth issue, 1953, of the *Cahiers internationaux de Sociologie.*

needs, as a starting point, sociological typology and its study of structures.[2] At this time I encountered Marx again, after many years of separation . . .

The same dialectical hyper-empiricism guided my research into *Les déterminismes sociaux et la liberté humaine* (1955). I tried to show how determinism and liberty might be interpenetrated and I studied sociologically the paths of liberty through the different social frameworks. The pluralism of social determinism that is always partial and its relative unification (through endless struggle and effort) within sociological determinism, while changing its formula with each type of global society, leave a wide area for the intervention of individual and collective human liberty in social life. In the same book I raised the problem of the multiplicity of social time, a problem to which I devoted my public lectures at the Sorbonne in the academic year 1957–58.[3]

Since my stay in the United States, my attention had been captivated by the problems raised by the sociology of knowledge. I had thought for a long time that it was impossible to approach the sociology of ethical life or the sociology of law in a sufficiently relativistic, realistic way without beginning with the sociology of knowledge. The way in which Scheler and Lévy-Bruhl raised this problem greatly attracted me. The study of the problem of symbols and signs as means of expression and diffusion strengthened my interest even more. The problem of ideology, which did not seem to me to have been sufficiently clarified from Marx to Mannheim thrust me in the same direction. In 1944–45, I gave a course on the sociology of knowledge at Harvard where I examined very closely all the concepts that had been formulated up to that time. Later on, I often raised this problem in my public

[2] Cf. my study 'Continuité et discontinuité en sociologie et en histoire' in *Annales*, 1957, and my article 'La crise de l'explication en sociologie', in the *Cahiers internationaux de Sociologie*, XXI, 1956. This subject is dealt with in a more detailed way in my course, *La multiplicité des temps sociaux*, 1958 (duplicated course, CDU).

[3] I show that social times unify and interpenetrate in hierarchies that vary according to the structures and types of global societies.

lectures at the Sorbonne and in my laboratory work at the Ecole Pratique des Hautes Etudes, as well as in several of my publications. I came to see that it was necessary to distinguish between different types of knowledge (perceptual knowledge of the external world; political knowledge; technical knowledge; scientific knowledge and philosophical knowledge) whose functional correlations with the social frameworks are of a *different intensity* and whose hierarchization in the *system of knowledge varies* as a function of the types of partial and global structures. By distinguishing within each *type* of knowledge the *forms* of knowledge that are accentuated differently as a function of the social structures (mystical and rational, intuitive and reflexive, conceptual and empirical, speculative and positive, symbolic and concrete, individual and collective), I arrived at numerous starting points for an empirical, concrete study of the problems of the sociology of knowledge. From then on, it was to cease competing with epistemology (to which in any case it can only pose new questions, without being competent to resolve them). Moreover, it was to cease beginning at the end, and would no longer approach in such a casual way the extremely delicate problem of placing in a sociological perspective the philosophical doctrines which survive the social structures in which they were created, and which can reappear every few centuries.

While I was editing my book *Introduction à la sociologie de la connaissance*,[4] I was tempted to take up again the problem of social classes—those supra-functional macrocosms of groups— a problem that I studied in a public lecture which was duplicated and should also be the subject of a book.

The method I used for the study of the problems in the sociology of knowledge led me to resume my research in an area

---

[4] My publications on this subject at this time were: *Initiation à la sociologie de la connaissance*, 1947 (duplicated course); 'Sociologie de la connaissance' in *L'Année sociologique* 1940–48, 1949; 'Structures sociales et systèmes de connaissance', in *Semaine sur la structure*, Centre de Synthèse, 1957; and 'Le problème de la sociologie de la connaissance', series of articles appearing in *La Revue philosophique* (1958–59).

of the sociology of moral life. In a public course given at the Sorbonne in 1956–57, while developing in detail a subject that I had already broached in 1948, I outlined the main points of my *Introduction à la sociologie de la vie morale*. All the types of moral life which I had come to distinguish (traditional morality, finalistic morality, morality of virtue, morality of *post facto* judgements, imperative morality, morality of ideal, symbolic images, morality of aspiration and morality of creation) were revealed to be involved in more intense relationships with the social reality than are the types of knowledge. Consequently, the sociology of moral life can establish functional correlations between social frameworks and types of morality on a much wider scale than is possible for the sociology of knowledge; furthermore, the microsociological elements and non-structured groups can serve as social frameworks here also. Obviously one arrives at the most concrete, most complete results by correlating moral life with social class and particularly with the types of global structures, by ascertaining the variation in the hierarchized systems of the types of moral life, as well as the change of emphasis in the *forms of morality* within them (rational or mystical, intuitive or reflexive, rigorist or natural which either atrophy or expand, are emulated or decay, collective or individual). Here again, this sociology of moral life, in appealing to empirical research does not compete with moral philosophy, but does present it with new problems.[5]

I have attempted to show as objectively as possible the path which led me to write my main works up to the present time. To conclude, I would like to point out that fate often made me go 'against the current' both in my thinking and work. The rhythm of my thinking was almost always out of step with fashion. I am thus 'excluded from the horde', by vocation so to speak. For the most part, French and American sociologists today think of me as a 'philosopher' who came to the wrong door; and the 'philo-

[5] Cf. my 'Réflexions sur la sociologie de la vie morale', in *Cahiers internationaux de Sociologie*, Vol. XXIV, 1958.

sophers' consider me as a 'traitor' who changed sides long ago.

However, this often painful position of isolation seems quite natural to me: my position implies the necessity for a close collaboration, not only between theory and empirical research, but also between sociology and philosophy, both relinquishing their dogmatism and imperialism. In watching and criticising each other, they can and must, while preserving their complete autonomy, ask each other basic questions to which only their incessant dialogue is capable of responding ... It is only when this attitude—which I attempted to make more precise in my article 'Sociologie et philosophie' written for *L'Encyclopédie française*, Vol. XIX, 1957—is accepted that I hope no longer to be banished from both clans.

Extracts from 'Mon itinéraire intellectuel ou l'exclu de la horde' in *L'homme et la société*, 1966.

II. REFERENCES

1. SAINT-SIMON

'What is important to me is neither to praise nor denigrate Saint-Simon's work, but to demonstrate the originality of his sociological contribution, as well as its limits.

'I. The originality of this author lies first of all in his conception of social reality and the science which studies it, a science which he called "the science of man", "social physiology" and sometimes "the science of liberty", emphasising the essentially dynamic character of sociology. "The coming together of man constitutes a real being", but this being is in no way biological; it is both collective and individual effort, material and spiritual production, action transforming nature, society and its participants, the transcendence of inherited structures, collective creation. The exteriorization of society that is always "in action" takes place through work.

'Society comes into being and creates itself, as well as its participants, its milieux, its tools, its organisations, its regimes, its cultural works. The social whole tends towards immanance; it resists projection on to an external object or a superior subject that certain regimes impose on it, constituting obstacles to its development. However, in its non-crystallised manifestations, society remains a "vast workshop", called upon to dominate not individuals, but nature.'

It has been observed, says Saint-Simon, 'that societies are subject to two moral forces which are of an equal intensity and which act alternately: one is the force of habit, the other is the force which results from the desire to experience novelty. After a certain time, habits necessarily become bad because they were started in a state of affairs which no longer corresponds to the needs of society. It is then that the need for novelty is felt, and this need which constitutes the real revolutionary state, remains until society is reconstituted' ... (*De le physiologie sociale*, 1812).

Thus '*the science of societies*' is also '*the science of liberty*' *and not only the science of régimes that are subject to determinism. 'If we want to be free, we must create our own freedom, and never expect it to come from elsewhere.*' It results in innovations, restiveness and revolutions which are, like their opposites, part of the social reality. Thus, according to Saint-Simon, because sociology is the study of society in action, it must take into consideration not only habits, customs, governments, regularities, but also collective aspirations, feelings, wishes, and restlessnesses, and must study the interpenetrations between social determinism and human liberty.

II. The actual character of social reality as effort, production, action, creation, and its expression in collective work, could not be revealed sufficiently clearly under theological, military and critical régimes (where respectively the priesthood, the military and jurist-metaphysicians held power). The modes of organizing production and work—conquest, theft, slavery, and thraldom for the profit of the idle governors being the basis of these régimes— arrested collective creative effort and 'camouflaged' the real main springs of social life. It is only at a time when production, by becoming completely pacifist, takes on an industrialized form and eliminates the idle for the benefit of the 'producers', that society regains possession of all its creative forces, and that all the camouflage concealing its characteristics is demystified.

Without using the term 'alienation' (borrowed by Marx from Feuerbach and through him from Hegel), Saint-Simon is alluding to exactly the same phenomenon; without mentioning 'ideology' (a term that Marx borrowed from Destutt de Tracy and Napoléon Bonaparte), he uncovered the conscious and unconscious camouflage surrounding the 'actual mainsprings of the society' which is not in possession of all the forces that it produces. If one omits the terminology, the difference between Saint-Simon, and Marx and Proudhon is restricted to the fact that the latter two are much more exacting than their predecessor with regard to the conditions which enable a society to recoup its forces . . .

Returning to Saint-Simon, it is as well to remember that in *Organisateur* (1819–20), he said quite clearly *that present day society is really a topsy-turvy world* and, in other works, he describes 'the class of jurists and metaphysicians'—this survival of the 'critical phase' of society—as the principal agent of 'camouflages', i.e. ideologies. But in the same *Organisateur*, Saint-Simon, with excessive optimism, again places his confidence in 'industrial régimes'—this 'society of workers' which includes capitalist-entrepreneurs intent on increasing their capital as well as that of the 'workers'—to overcome alienations and ideologies; in fact, in 'industrial régimes', 'everything tends naturally towards order, disorder in the last analysis always coming from the idle' . . . It was only later that Saint-Simon arrived at a clearer awareness of the tensions possible between the social classes within the category of 'producers' . . .

III. Collective human effort is both material and spiritual. These two aspects are inseparably linked in the life of societies, whose 'capacity for spiritualism and materialism is equal'. 'I shall prove', said Saint-Simon, 'that until the present time we have called spiritualist those things that should have been called materialist, and materialist those that should have been called spiritualist. Surely embodying an abstraction is being materialist? Extracting an idea from existence, is that not being spiritualist?' This sentence from *Travail sur la gravitation* (1813), referred to by Marx,[1] is Saint-Simon's way of saying that in concrete society

---

[1] Cf. his posthumous work *Critique de la philosophie de l'Etat de Hegel*, 1842: 'Abstract spiritualism is abstract materialism; abstract materialism is spiritualism of matter' (*Oeuvres philos.*, Vol. IV, Fr. trans. Molitor, p 183).

in action, material and spiritual production are interpenetrated and that if ordinarily they develop simultaneously, they can also enter into conflict. This is why Saint-Simon can state both 'that there is no society without common ideas' and that 'morality is the necessary bond in society', and that 'it is in industry that in the last analysis all the real forces of society reside' (*L'Industrie*, Vol. II and Vol. III, 1817). He states that 'materal production transforms ownership' (for example, 'industrial ownership, separate, independent and eventually the rival of territorial ownership'); now, 'the form of government is only a form, and the constitution of membership is fundamental. Therefore, it is this constitution which is the foundation of the social structure.' Thus, he had already written in *De la réorganisation européenne* (1814): 'There can be no change in the social order without a change in ownership.'

However, he states elsewhere that 'the production of ideas occurs in the constitution of any society', and, exaggerating his case somewhat, he says, that 'every social régime is an application of a philosophical system, and consequently it is impossible to set up a new régime without having first established a new philosophical system to which it must correspond'. In reading Saint-Simon carefully, one cannot fail to notice that he sees the economy, ownership, political régimes, moral values and ideas, intellectual ideas, and systems of knowledge as only partial manifestations of the *total social activity*, in which they have to be situated in order to be understood and explained. It was not in vain that he wrote: '*At all times and in every society, one finds a correspondence between social institutions and moral ideas.*' (*L'industrie*, Vol. III, 1817.) How could it be otherwise, given that 'the origin of morality is necessarily merged with the origin of society'? (*ibid.*). The same is true for intellectual ideas, for knowledge, particularly in the sciences, their classifications and their various unifications, and also for philosophy. One of the missions of sociology or 'social physiology' is to look for the correspondence not only between this 'spiritual production' and 'material production', but also the whole of society distinguished according to its different 'régimes' or types.

IV. The problem that Saint-Simon raised here, which he had suggested in his earliest work, is deeper and has wider implications because of the fact that 'spoken and written' signs occur in the social reality. 'The line of demarcation', he said in the *Introduction aux travaux scientifiques du dix-neuvième siècle*, Vol. II, 1808, 'between man's intelligence and animal instinct was clearly drawn only after the formation of the conventional *system* of spoken and written *signs*'. And he added, in the *Introduction à la philosophie du dix-neuvième siècle*, 1810: 'The earliest men were scarcely superior in intelligence to the other animals,' but they raised themselves to another level by a 'system of signs' which is one element of human society. 'We do not know the name of the people who organised the sign system; but we are certain that it existed prior to the Egyptians.' In short, in creating itself, society also created signs, just as it created techniques ('the system of arts and crafts'), fine arts, moral values and ideas, mathematical and physical sciences, and biological physiology first of all, then *social physiology or the science of man* which is the order of the day in 'industrial society'.

Saint-Simon was a believer in a clear opposition between the natural world and the social world. He wrote in the aforementioned *Introduction aux travaux scientifiques*: 'There exist two distinct things: *what is Us; what is external to Us. The action of Us on what is external to Us. The action of what is external to Us on Us.* This division is much greater than the division between the faculties of our intelligence, which is better taken as a mere sub-division.'

V. Thus, Saint-Simon was faced with a new problem. It was not only a question of the sociology of knowledge and moral life, but also the sociology of signs and, I would add, symbols, as well as the sociology of technical models. Unfortunately, Saint-Simon did not develop his views on these questions which might have led him to distinguish several depth levels of social reality and to study the variations in their importance in different types of societies.

He restricted himself to considering knowledge and moral life. In contrast to Condorcet and Comte, Saint-Simon did not attribute any primacy to knowledge, but sought to show that its position and its characteristics depended on the real social frameworks of which it is a part. Thus, the predominance of theological knowledge corresponds to military régimes; the predominance of metaphysical knowledge to intermediary 'critical régimes'; the predominance of technical knowledge, for which scientific knowledge is merely a substitute, to fully developed industrial régimes. The first system of knowledge corresponds to the privileged role of the idle and unemployed class—soldiers and priests. The second system of knowledge is parallel to the domination by the class of 'jurists and metaphysicians', maintained by idle property owners. Finally, the third system of knowledge presupposes the coming to power of the 'producers'. It is under this régime that the science of man or sociology is promoted.

Similarly, the orientation of moral life is related to the types of societies. Under military régimes 'heavenly morality' predominates, guided by the priests. Intermediary, critical régimes further the success of utilitarian, rational morality inspired by the 'jurists and metaphysicians'. These two moralities, the one heavenly and the other terrestrial, are inegalitarian; they do not consider men as co-operating partners, but divide them into governors and governed. Under developed industrial régimes morality is attached to production and work; it becomes a morality of co-operating workers in partnership. To this, *Le nouveau Christianisme* adds the morality of charity, fraternity and love, based on a pantheistic humanism, which completes the morality of the producers in favour of the proletariat—'the largest and poorest class' whose existence and possible enslavement to the 'industrial hierarchy' Saint-Simon finally discovered. Obviously Saint-Simon was here by-passing the obvious problems involved in a sociology of moral life, which he clearly recognized, in order to build up a moral philosophy. He vainly expected it to resolve the internal, endless contradictions of his technocratic 'industrial pyramid'—the stumbling block in his socio-political doctrine.

VI. Coming back to what should be called the *sociology* of Saint-Simon, we ought to consider his conception of the relationship between State and economic society. This relationship depends on the character of the economic society. The State is necessary for governing economic society, both under military régimes and in the intermediary 'critical period' (prolonged by jurists and metaphysicians) when industry, despite its development, remains in an anarchic state and is not effectively organized. On the other hand, the decay of the State is inevitable when 'the producers' (entrepreneurs, employers and workers) manage to control industry: when 'the administration of things replaces the government of people'. The sociologist will be less interested in this utopian prediction of the dissolution of the State in economic society—with Fichte as Saint-Simon's predecessor, Proudhon and Marx as successors in making the prediction —than in all the implications which underlie it.

First, Saint-Simon sees the State as a manifestation of the domination of one class over the others and usually it is the least productive, most idle class: first the military class, then the class of 'jurists and metaphysicians', and finally the 'bourgeois' class —investors, idle owners of capital and the means of production. Then Saint-Simon notes that the State can artificially dominate an economic society, by making itself partially independent and thus impeding its development. This is precisely what happens when, after the industrial régime has been established, classes who have lost all useful social function (for example, nobles, jurists, idle bourgeois-property-owners) prevent the industrial régime from attaining full strength by refusing power to the 'producers'. Sooner or later, however, the economic society ends up by overthrowing the retrograde political régime, especially since the economic society represents better than any State the global society of which the political régime is only a narrow sector.

This leads us to the final aspect of the opposition that Saint-Simon established between State and economic society. The State appears to him as a crystallised organization which, although in the last resort it depends on global collective activity, can easily be detached from it, pressurizes it, and often plays the role of an obstacle to live social forces, thus hindering social life. Saint-Simon here touches on the problem of the relationship between the total social phenomenon, its structure and its organization, as well as the problem of the relationship between total social phenomena and global and partial structures. But he does not analyse the complexity of these relationships and forgets that the economic society also has its organizations and its hierarchies. Elsewhere he uses and abuses these organizations and hierarchies, by attributing 'spontaneity' to 'industry'.

In the famous 'Parabole' in *L'Organisateur* which puts forward the supposition that the sudden disappearance of Statist organization would not be detrimental since industrial society develops spontaneously and thus independently of the governmental apparatus, that in the end the 'producers' might well not notice that the men representing the framework of the State had disappeared, Saint-Simon discusses all aspects of his conception of the relationships between State and economic society. He particularly emphasizes the last element that I mentioned. Obviously, he combines it with a dogmatic, arbitrary evaluation of 'industry'. thus departing from sociology to a socio-political doctrine and a philosophy of history which aims at liberating humanity from the yoke of the State . . .

Extract from C. H. de Saint-Simon, *La physiologie sociale, Oeuvres choisies*, Introduction and notes by Georges Gurvitch, Paris, Presses Universitaires de France, 1965.

E

2. PROUDHON

This brings us on to Proudhon's general conception of social reality. According to him, it reveals four main aspects or, to use my own terminology, four levels or stages:

(1) Social existence appears first of all in the guise of 'collective forces' that are irreducible to individual forces; the former are 'immanent in society in the same way as attraction is to matter'. When the society, particular groups, including the State, and classes organize themselves, their collective forces become *power*, whether it be political, economic or social power (*ibid.*, pp. 261–262).[2] These collective forces and powers, however intense they may be, do not directly involve either justice or law or ideal. But they may produce and refine them, or they may decline, become perverted or alienated. It is in this way that, under a capitalist régime, economic collective forces are alienated from the bosses who exploit the workers. It is also in this way that the political collective forces are alienated from the authoritarian State which, instead of serving justice, is subordinated to the interest of the dominant classes, which were once landowners, now the bourgeoisie.

But the social reality cannot be reduced merely to the play of collective forces. 'Materialism' said Proudhon in his work *De la capacité politique des classes ouvrières*, 'in relation to society is absurd, for the collective forces can create ideas and values which are integrated in it and then become capable of guiding them. This is particularly the case of collective work in its struggle against alienation.

(2) These considerations lead us to the second aspect of social existence, intermediary between the collective forces and the ideas and values which can arise from them (particularly the idea of justice). It concerns regulation by a law capable of balancing the conflicts so often engendered by collective forces. Proudhon

[2] P. J. Proudhon, *De la justice* ... Vol. II, 1858.

is certainly too much of a jurist: in the complexity of social reality, he attributes an over-important role to law, particularly to egalitarian, reciprocal law, on the one hand, and to autonomous, spontaneous social law on the other. He contrasts them with individualist law and Statist law derived from traditional Roman law.

To be fair to Proudhon and to do him credit, one might perhaps replace the term 'law' by 'social regulation' or 'social control', used by American sociologists. It concerns models, rules, signs, signals, symbols of different kinds which abound in all social reality. One must then commend Proudhon for having enriched the social reality and for having emphasized the fact that it includes not only collective forces, but also social regulations that arise out of these forces and that these two levels are in many dialectical relationships of whose complexity he was aware.

However, Proudhon considers—and this shows that he did not succeed in completely going beyond his initial rationalism—that the more social regulations succeed in guiding the collective forces from which they are derived, the more likely it is that social justice will triumph in a society or group. But in order to bring about this situation, at least partially, there have to be, according to Proudhon, two conditions: (a) the clear assertion of the ideas and values produced by action and, more specifically, by collective work in the process of disalienation; (b) the recognition of the collective consciousness, which Proudhon always equates with 'collective reason'.

(3) The third aspect or stage of social reality is comprised therefore of collective ideas and values, whose ideals are based on affectivity; when united with the idea of justice, these ideals strengthen revolutionary energy; without this link they lead to decadence.

(4) The preceding aspects lead on to the fourth level, described by Proudhon as 'common consciousness' or 'social consciousness' and which he wrongly equated with 'collective reason', 'social spirit' or 'public reason'. He discusses it throughout his book and

especially in the *Septième étude*, devoted to *Idées*. Proudhon is anxious about the 'corruption of public reason' by the absolute and observes that the bourgeois revolution made this public reason immanent and free, but not sufficiently efficacious. Social revolution alone will make it predominant. Elsewhere Proudhon emphasizes the main difference which exists between collective reason and individual reason (*ibid.*, p. 250). 'Collective reason makes no deductions'; it is essentially practical, but this does not prevent it from becoming theoretical too. It innovates and helps to create; it explodes in revolutions and will lead to the triumph of social justice in the future. 'I think it useless to insist on this fundamental distinction between individual and collective reason, the former essentially absolutist, the second antipathetic to all absolutism.' (*ibid.*, p. 253.)

Collective reason reveals that 'society, the epitome of moral being *par excellence*, differs essentially from living (individual) beings, in whom the subordination of the organs is the very law of existence. This is why society repudiates any idea of hierarchy, as expressed in the statement: 'all men are equal in dignity through nature and must become equivalent from the point of view of their conditions and their dignity' (*ibid.*, p. 265). 'It is therefore individual, absolutist, reason, proceeding through genesis and syllogism which continually tends to synthesise society through the subordination of people, functions, and characteristics; whereas collective reason, always seeking to eliminate the absolute, invariably proceeds by formulations that relate to the society that it represents and energetically denies all systems.' (p. 267.)

'The organ of collective reason is the same as that of the collective force; it is the working, teaching group; the industrial, scientific, artistic company; the academies, schools, municipalities; the national Assembly, the club, the jury' (p. 270). In summary, it is any particular group, as well as any social class, or any global society, provided that the circumstances lend themselves to it. Proudhon attributes to collective reason an action that is both pragmatic and moralizing (hence his famous statement, taken from a letter to Cournot: 'Morality is a revelation of the collective to the individual'); he does not find this capacity to a comparable degree in individual reason. One can therefore say that ideas return to the action which gave rise to them through the intermediary of collective, essentially pragmatic reason.

Proudhon does not invest collective reason with transcendence, or the characteristic of 'logos', or the possibility of being perceived or perceiving intuitively. Thus, he does not specify how 'collective reason' becomes aware of the ideas and values that arise from action and more directly from collective work. Its role as clarificator and innovator, the difference even between its contents or products and collective effort remain obscure. This is the weak point of Proudhon's analysis, the open door to many misunderstandings. So much so that Proudhon's texts sometimes contain strains of Rousseau's 'general will' that he criticized so much. Proudhon writes: 'When two or more men are asked to give opposite views on a question, the result is that in turn they have to produce for each other from their own subjectivity, i.e. the absolute that the self affirms and which he represents, a common way of seeing, which in no way resembles, in either substance or form, what would otherwise have been their individual way of thinking' (*ibid.*, p. 261). Thus, sometimes, 'collective reason is made up of the equation or reciprocal balance of individual thoughts' (*ibid.*, p. 265). Through its equations we see collective reason constantly destroying the system formed by the coalition of particular reasons; therefore, it is not only different, it is superior to all of them' (*ibid.*, p. 268). This position is close to Durkheim's.

Thus, one might wonder if Proudhon's discussion of 'collective reason' does not finally lead him to an impasse. The confusion between 'collective consciousness' and 'collective reason', the barely concealed primacy attributed to both of them over collective forces and the social regulations that they produce, the lack

of precision about the relationships of collective consciousness
and reason with ideas and values, and lastly the absence of a
pertinent analysis of the development of 'collective reason' from
action—all undeniably reduce the efficacy of the realist pragmatism that Proudhon wanted to promote.

However, it should not be forgotten that Proudhon is essentially a supporter of the dialectic, and primarily the dialectic of
the movement of social reality. 'Collective consciousness' and
'collective reason' are a part of this dialectic. All the aspects or
stages of social reality, including 'collective reason', are dialecticized. From this point of view, 'collective reason' is only one
part of the 'totalisation' of social life. Certainly the term 'collective reason' is unfortunate, especially since it is hard to know
exactly what Proudhon meant and whether he really thought of
'reason' in the usual sense of the word. What is certain, however, is that Proudhon wanted to arrive at a *consistent pragmatic
relativism* in sociology, that was both *realistic* and *dialectical*,
but that he did not always have the means, and, moreover, that
he was betrayed by his own terminology. We should at least
recognize that his intentions were sound, even if he did not completely succeed in bringing them about.

Let me summarize the main characteristics of Proudhon's
sociology that I have just discussed, so that they can be subjected
to a critical analysis.

I. Social reality is multiform and pluridimensional. Its different
stages, levels (or aspects) are: collective forces; law, and more
broadly, social regulations (signs, models, rules, symbols); justice
and the ideal, which are sometimes in conflict, sometimes in
harmony; and lastly 'collective reason', equated with collective
consciousness.

II. This social reality constitutes a totality or, more accurately, it
is involved in a dialectical movement of 'totalisation'. The basis
of this reality is effort, collective action, whose richest manifestation is work, which involves all the above mentioned dimensions.
It is through collective work that collective forces penetrate all

levels of the social totality. But this penetration is linked to the stages in disalienation from work, which makes successive revolutions necessary.

III. Collective spontaneity plays an essential role, and it is in revolutions that this is best demonstrated. Moreover, without it, neither collective forces, nor work, nor social regulations, nor justice, nor collective reason, nor collective liberty, linked to the will, could function.

IV. There exists in every society, a multiplicity of groups, and, under the capitalist régime, social classes arise when the proletariat is united with the peasantry and opposed to the bourgeoisie. Their struggle tends towards social revolution. This is capable not only of disalienating work, but of transforming international wars into battles aimed at subjugating nature.

V. Sociological pluralism, revealed in the existence of multiple groups (and often different classes) and in conflicts between the State and the economic society, is required by the facts.

VI. In so far as work remains alienated, the whole of social reality in all its stages, as well as the collective forces, are monopolized by the owning classes, particularly by industrial bosses and high finance.

VII. Progress is the victory of collective liberty, linked to the collective will which, due to revolutions, brings about the triumph of collective reason and justice coupled with an affective ideal. It also appeals for new revolutions. There is never anything automatic or fatalistic about progress. Regression, decadence, 'retrogression' are as real as progress and are always possible in society, groups and social classes.

VIII. Ideas, values, justice, and 'collective reason' derived from and guiding the collective forces through a process of refinement come mainly from action and work in the course of disalienation, and must return to action. They degenerate when they lose contact with action and when they are not realized in struggle, effort, work, creation and revolution.

IX. Proudhon's sociological theory risks seeming incomprehensible if one does not take into account the depth and complexity of his dialectic, which cannot be reduced either to the mere search for insoluble antinomies, nor to equilibria. Despite not showing it clearly, Proudhon offers a diversified dialectic of the movement of social reality, which is sometimes manifested in complementarity, sometimes in mutual involvement, sometimes in reciprocity of perspectives. The dialectic leads to ever-renewed and ever-renewing experiences.

Extract from G. Gurvitch, *Proudhon*, Paris, Presses Universitaires de France, 1965.

3. MARX

I shall try to summarize Marx's dialectic as objectively as possible, so that a critical appreciation can be made.

Marx sought an appropriate term to express more clearly that the dialectic is first and foremost the actual movement of economic, social and historical reality (which, however, are one and the same reality, i.e. society in action). It is only incidentally, in a secondary way, also a method. He particularly needed an appropriate term since he contrasted his dialectic both with that of Hegel, who linked the fate of the dialectic to his mystical spiritualism, and that of Plato for whom the dialectic was but one method used in considering eternal ideas, and also with that of Proudhon, whom he accused of conceding too much both to the Platonic and the Hegelian dialectic.

The young Marx described his own position in *La Sainte Famille* (Vol. II, 1844), as a *realist humanism*. One could say that the most appropriate description of his dialectual orientation would be the *dialectic of realist humanism*, because it emphasizes the fact that everything which springs from human reality as real movement and as awareness of this movement is dialectical. Marx also said that his dialectic is to be seen, among other things, in the 'new materialism' or 'practical materialism' which had nothing in common with the old materialism. He added that this dialectic also appears in 'historiography with a materialist basis', without suggesting that they are the only possible expressions of his dialectic, and specified that the 'new materialism' coincides with humanism (Vol. II, p. 223). However, this choice of terms turned out to be unfortunate, not only because it led Engels and popular Marxism to talk about 'economic materialism' and 'dialectical materialism'—which Marx never thought of in any phase of his development—but especially because, for him, the dialectic was linked to '*social praxis*' where '*materialism and spiritualism are no longer in opposition*', to use his own words.

This is true since, on the one hand, societies are *totalities*, which include both material productive forces, the relationships of production, real (individual and collective) consciousness, as well as its works and ideology; on the other hand, one of the essential aspects of the dialectical movement is made up of *alienations* which, if they appear in different forms, have for the most part only a slight relationship to the material element of society. Similarly, at that time, Marx insisted on the fact that 'the mode of common action is itself a productive force' (*Idéol. all.*, 1845, Vol. VII, p. 167) and that 'of all the instruments of production, the greatest productive power is the revolutionary class itself' (*Misère de la philosophie*, 1847, 1946 ed., p. 135). This amounts to saying that the dialectic of the productive forces, as well as the dialectic of the class struggle and revolutions involves class consciousness, aspirations, ideals, and cultural works at the same time as material forces. Marx said so in *L'Idéologie allemande* (Vol. VI, p. 164): 'The production of ideas, representations and consciousness, is first and foremost directly involved in the material activity of men' and is the language of life (pp. 156–7).

One should not therefore be surprised to read in *Economie politique et philosophie* (1844): 'It is only in the social state that subjectivism and objectivism, spiritualism and materialism, activity and passivity cease being in opposition and consequently lose their reason for existence. It can be seen that the solution to theoretical oppositions is possible only in a practical way through the practical energy of man in society' Vol. VI, pp. 34–35). Society is 'human reality whose manifestations are as varied as human determinations and activities' (*ibid.*, p. 29). In this area, 'thinking and being are . . . both different and the same' (*ibid.*, p. 28). It concerns a 'humanism originating in itself, positive humanism' (*ibid.*, p. 86), and it is this humanism which is dialectical, both in being and thinking, which are themselves in a dialectical relationship. This is why Marx complains in *La Sainte Famille* (1845), 'That after the old opposition between spiritualism and materialism had been completely put aside . . . , (neo-Hegelian) criticism again makes it the fundamental dogma, in a most repugnant form, and causes the German-Christian spirit to triumph.' (Vol. II, p. 167.)

The dialectic appropriate to realist humanism extends its methodological repercussions into the problem of relationships between natural and human sciences. Their dialectic, acording to the young Marx, leads to the transcendence of the naturalist orientation in the human sciences. 'The human being of nature exists only for the social man; for it is only there that nature exists for him as a link with man, as existence for others and as existence of others for him.' 'Society is therefore the perfect consubstantiality of man with nature, . . . the realisation of the naturalism of man and the humanism of nature' (Vol. VI, p. 26). Thus, it is due to society that 'perfect naturalism is humanism and perfect humanism naturalism' (p. 23). If 'the natural sciences have intervened in the life of man and have transformed it' (p. 38), 'the science of man will encompass the natural sciences' (p. 36). This dialectic therefore leads to the observation that the human and the social intervene in nature, and more particularly in the natural sciences, for 'all science is a practical social activity and involves a strong human coefficient' (Thèses sur Feuerbach, *Idéol. all.*, pp. 141–4). It was therefore through the mediation of social praxis and sociology that the young Marx foresaw the application of the dialectic to the natural sciences . . .

Elsewhere, added Marx in *La Sainte Famille* (Vol. II, pp. 234–5), 'if man draws all his knowledge from the physical world, it is important to organise this world in such a way that man encounters and assimilates what is really human, that he knows himself as man' (*ibid.*, p. 234). '*If man is formed by circumstances, circumstances must be humanely formed. If man is, by nature, sociable, he can develop his true nature only in society.*' (*ibid.*, p. 235.) The young Marx therefore rejected in the name of his *dialectical humanist realism* not only materialism, but also an over-strict and rigorous determinism. He appealed to society and man *in action*.

All these points are taken up again in the famous 'Thèses sur Feuerbach' which provide the introduction to the *Idéologie allemande*, dating from 1845, and published in 1932. It should be said that the 'Thèses' were known well before then, due to the fact that Engels added them to his book: *Ludwig Feuerbach et la fin de la philosophie classique allemande* (1886). The *troisiéme thèse* went further than *La Sainte Famille* on the subject of materialist determinism: 'The materialist doctrine', we read here, 'which claims that men are products of circumstances and education, that, consequently, changed men are products of other circumstances and a different education, forgets that it is precisely men who change circumstances and that the educator himself needs to be educated.' This is why, writes Marx in the *première thèse*, 'the principle mistake of all past materialism, including Feuerbach's, is that the object, reality, the tangible world are considered only in the form of object or intuition, but not as concrete human activity, as practice. This explains why the active side was developed by idealism in opposition to materialism, but only abstractly, for idealism does not know real concrete activity as such.' And in the *quatrième thèse*: 'The fact that the secular foundation is detached from itself and establishes an independent empire in the clouds as an independent kingdom, can only be explained by this other fact, that this foundation . . . lacks cohesion and is in contradiction with itself. It is necessary, consequently, that this foundation be understood in its contradiction as well as revolutionised in practice.' *Huitième thèse*: 'All social life is essentially praxis.' All problems find 'their rational solution in human practice and in the understanding of this practice'. *Neuvième et dixième thèses*: 'The new materialism includes materiality as practical activity'; its 'point of view is human society or social humanity'.

It can be clearly seen that the word materialism is badly chosen, for it concerns a dialectical realist humanism which is totally practical. The young Marx himself emphasized this strongly:[3] 'Man produces man, himself and the other man' (p. 25). Is this 'production of man through human work' uniquely material? No, for through their content and exercise 'activity and spirit are, according to the manner of their existence, sociability, social activity and social spirit' (p. 26). 'Law, morality, science, the spirit, etc., are only particular modes of production' (p. 24). It is therefore, from all the evidence, not materialism, but dialectical humanist realism.

In fact, the term 'new materialism' can be explained only by historical reasons. It is used only as a protest against the theological spiritualism of Hegel and the neo-Hegelians, and refers to Feuerbach who was already considered a materialist. Furthermore, Marx said so directly in the introduction to *La Sainte Famille* (Vol. II, p. 9): 'Realist humanism has no more dangerous enemy in Germany than spiritualism or speculative idealism which puts "consciousness" or "spirit" in the place of the real man.' He repeated this observation in another form and with different emphasis (to be dealt with later) in his analysis in the preface to the second edition of the first volume of *Capital*: 'My dialectical method does not merely differ from the Hegelian

[3] Cf. *Economie politique et philosophie, op. cit.*, Vol. VI.

method as far as the basis is concerned, it is the direct opposite of it. For Hegel, the process of thought, which he makes into an autonomous subject, in the name of idea, is the creator of the reality which is only the external phenomenon.' In order to break 'the mystification in which Hegel's dialectic ends, and which only serves to transform what exists', it is necessary to 'turn it over', to 'stand it back on its feet', for it has a 'topsy turvy meaning' and 'is standing on its head'. It is therefore in opposition to Hegelian spiritualist mystification (which passes as dialectic) that Marx accepts the unfortunate term 'materialism', even though this term in no way expresses his thinking.

I shall try to show that even when Marx in the *Contribution à la critique de l'économie politique* (1859), hardened his positions by attributing primacy to the material productive forces, in stating that 'the anatomy of society is to be found in the economy' and in projecting most cultural works into the 'ideological superstructures', he does not therefore become a materialist, but is simply characterizing a particular type of society— capitalist society—and is seeking landmarks for reconstituting the totality of society which is always, for him, much more than its economy. The dialectical movement of society modifies the characteristics of the economy.

Even if he does not always clearly differentiate between them, Marx considers at least seven dialectical movements in the social reality. I feel it is essential to go over them:

(1) First, there is the dialectic of revolutionary syntheses.

(2) Then, the dialectic between the productive forces, the relationships of production, consciousness, cultural works and ideologies, a dialectic that in my own terminology, I describe as the dialectic of the depth levels of social reality.

(3) Thirdly, the dialectic of social classes and their struggle, changes in their role, their number and their internal divisions.

(4) Then, the dialectic of *alienations*, assuming different meanings and forms, and being particularly strengthened under capitalist régimes.

(5) The dialectic of economic life in general and the capitalist economy in particular.

(6) One of the aspects of this is the dialectic between societies as totalities and their economies as sectors of these totalities, which may also lead to a dialectic between economic science and sociology.

(7) The dialectic of historical movement crowns the whole edifice. This tends to encompass all other dialectics, but, however, provokes in Marx himself a dialectic between sociology and historical knowledge or science of history.

Extract from G. Gurvitch, *Dialectique et sociologie*, Paris, Flammarion, 1962.

III. SOCIOLOGICAL DEVELOPMENT

1. DIALECTICAL HYPER-EMPIRICISM

Having been unable to accept any interpretation of the dialectic, not even those which seem closest to my own research, I find myself under an obligation to bring together my negations, in the hope that they will lead to something positive. The impenitent, intransigent dialectic, the untamed dialectic, can be neither ascendent nor descendent, nor both together. It can lead neither to salvation, nor to despair nor to salvation via despair. It offers no panacea for the reconciliation of humanity with itself. It can be neither spiritualist nor materialist, nor mystical. It cannot favour any type of knowledge, either scientific, philosophical or common sense, etc. It cannot be projected either into consciousness or being, the relationships between the two being themselves dialectical and necessarily dialecticized. Consciousness can be considered as part of being, imbedded in being, and being can be considered as present in consciousness without being given over to it. The cause of the dialectic is lost in advance if it begins by allying itself with a particular philosophical or scientific position. It precedes them all, it prepares the way for them by frustrating dogmatization, facile solutions, conscious or unconscious sublimation. 'The dialectic is therefore a path. Furthermore, in the very word dialectic, there is the idea of *dia*, through; the dialectic is a path rather than the point of departure or the point of arrival. Perhaps the dialectic is properly speaking a method.'[1] But what is it then? A movement of being, of reality? Certainly either, and this takes us even further. Going

[1] Cf. Jean Wahl, *Traité de métaphysique*, 1953, pp. 696–7.

to extremes one could say that the dialectic cannot be merely a method, not merely a real movement for this reason alone, that it requires the relationships between method and reality (objectifiable and objectified reality) to be dialecticized themselves. All reality that we can know or even perceive is already dialecticized through the very fact of collective and individual human intervention. This human existence, whether revealed through methods or outside the field of method—the usual case—makes everything that it touches dialectical, including all the so-called (natural, technical, cultural) 'milieux' which surround it and which are both its products and its producers.

The dialectic is therefore the way chosen by the acting human being in order to perceive real changing totalities which bear his imprint directly or indirectly. This includes human reality itself as well as the varying relationships between human reality and the whole of the real being. This involves a series of degrees of intensity of the dialectic which, to take scientific knowledge as an example, is more keenly felt in the human sciences than in the natural sciences, and in sociology more strongly than in the other human sciences. Furthermore, at different historical turning points in thought or existence, the importance of the dialectic varies and is differently accentuated.

But, one might say, if this is so, would it not be falling into a flagrant contradiction in wanting to link the fate of the dialectic to *empiricism*? For, even when it is extended, radical, and integral, empiricism is still a preconceived philosophical position which is justified by the mediation of the dialectic. One could respond in two ways to this objection.

The dialectic is a pathway leading not to empiricism, in the historical sense of the term, but to infinitely varied experiences whose very frames of reference are rendered flexible and are constantly being renewed. These dynamic explosive experiences are certainly not possible without penetration by the dialectic, without the dialecticization of everything that is experienced and known, a dialecticization, which thus prevents them from being dogmatized. It is not therefore a matter of super-imposing a new empiricism on the dialectic, but of fusing the continual demolition of concepts with perceptions whose comings and goings are changeable and contingent. It is in this sense that one might say that the impenitent, intransigent dialectic is hyper-empiricist, and that experience which is constantly modifying its very foundations immanently involves a dialectic.

Neither should it be forgotten that the fate of empiricism in the history of philosophy is somewhat analogous to the fate of the dialectic. Empiricism in its original inspiration was not a philosophical position, but a preliminary clearing of the ground, a destruction of all that was directly or indirectly opposed to contact with the vicissitudes of reality. Like the dialectic, empiricism was sidetracked from its vocation by the apologetic, tame character that was attributed to it. It too was transformed into an instrument for justifying preconceived theses, which in reality were external to it. This was so for all the many different kinds of empiricism that were ever preached. My observation is accurate not only for the classical forms of empiricism: the defence of isolated sensations and their mechanical combinations in Condillac; the defence of thought that directs sensations through the intermediary of tangible associations in Locke and Hume; the glorification of 'given, observed facts' in a scientific induction which can never be closed, in Mill and other positivists, etc. This observation also turns out to be accurate for the more refined, more recent forms of empiricism: 'the immediate' that one presupposes to be attained—either in religious and mystical experience (W. James), or in 'affective experience' (Rauh and Scheler) or in the 'flux of neotic experience' and 'experience of the transcendental I' (Husserl) or in 'existential experience'—is merely a preconceived statement. On the one hand, the 'immediate' and the 'constructed' are merely extreme cases, infinite tasks that we can never accomplish. We only experience the intermediary spheres, the 'mediates' going in

F

opposite directions. Lived experience, like constructed experience places us in inextricable webs of 'mediations of the immediate' and 'immediations of the mediate': we therefore find ourselves in lived experience, as elsewhere, plunging deep into the dialectic. On the other hand, James' pluralist pantheism, Bergson's creative duration, Scheler's objective values or Rauh's pragmatic values, Husserl's essences or his transcendental I, 'existence' in its different interpretations, are only constructions artificially introduced into 'the experience of the immediate', or into actual experience so that they can be rediscovered there later.

As soon as one expresses a certain univocal theory of experience so that it might serve a certain cause, whether one calls it sensualism, associationism, scientific positivism, criticism, mysticism, pragmatism, phenomenology or existentialism, one distorts it, one arrests this experience, one destroys the unforseeableness, the infinite variety, and the unexpectedness of its very frameworks by using it as a standard of validation for a preconceived position. Now, what makes experience so close to the dialectic which is its driving force, so to speak, is that it is always breaking its own frames of reference. It is like a veritable Proteus: it escapes us when we think we have it, we are duped by it when we believe we have discovered its secret, we are victims of it when we think we are rid of it, even if this is only for a moment . . .

Moreover, one should not forget another striking affinity between experience and dialectic: they are both attached to the *human*, to everything that represents human action, surroundings, and accoutrements, everything that is 'contaminated' by the human. Experience is always human, it is never either infrahuman or super-human; it is the effort of man, group, and society to direct themselves in the world, to adapt themselves, to change themselves; this is the collective and individual 'praxis', which the young Marx emphasized. Even scientific experience, not only in the social sciences but in the natural sciences remains essentially 'human experience' and bears the imprint of human and social repercussions on nature. One sees therefore how dialectical hyper-empiricism is human and how the human is hyper-empirical and dialectical *par excellence.*

Two questions arise before we can manage to specify the main technical procedures of dialectical hyper-empiricism, especially in their applications to sociology, which I consider to be the essential task of this study. First, what would be the most striking direct results of this orientation? And then, what relationship would this orientation have to other philosophical and scientific positions?

In answer to the first question, the most indisputable consequences of dialectical hyper-empiricism seem to be the following:

(A) It leads to super-relativism, by frustrating conscious or unconscious idealization, sublimation or dogmatization of the present, past or future circumstances, by hindering facile solutions and by making relativism and historicism themselves relative.

(B) It dialecticizes all relationships between subject and object, consciousness and being, significance and signified, symbol and symbolized, act and work, mediate and immediate, by showing the infinite variety in their appearance, their intermediary degrees, their emphases, their dimensions, their implications, and finally, by accentuating disturbance in the relationships themselves.

(C) It replaces synthesis, unification, elevation (*Aufheben*) and even reconciliation, harmonization and equilibrium with new, unforeseeable, unexpected experiences which open up new abysses at every corner and provide the most dangerous surprises where everything is brought into question.

(D) It reveals the multi-dimensionality of all knowable reality; it dialecticizes the relationship between the object of a science and reality; it shows the conditional character of any science whose field depends on a chosen frame of reference, and it makes this increasingly more flexible.

(E) It dialecticizes the relationships between the natural sciences and human sciences, between particular social sciences and sociology, as well as its different branches, between scientific knowledge and philosophical knowledge. It highlights the mobility of partial interpretations between natural sciences and human sciences, between sociology and social sciences, and between sciences and philosophy. It reveals the almost infinite flexibility and perpetual fluctuations of these interpenetrations, permitting a multiplicity of degrees which depend on the circumstances within these disciplines ... Here I shall stop enumerating the primary consequences of dialectical hyper-empiricism, for I mention them only by way of examples that could obviously be multiplied indefinitely.

As for the relationships between dialectical hyper-empiricism and particular philosophical and scientific doctrines, no decisive solution seems possible. This orientation excludes certain doctrines such as idealism, rationalism, criticism, sensualism, positivism, and even spiritualism and materialism. It seems that it can be integrated *post factum* into certain others such as absolute realism, heroic humanism, pragmatism, the theory of the perpetual renewal of reason, voluntarism, existentialism, phenomenology, or a broad intuitionism, and even mysticism of various kinds. But the vocation of a dialectical hyper-empiricism is to facilitate and to promote the birth of new philosophical doctrines, by excluding dogmatism, and tendencies to restriction and division. Likewise, in the sciences, this orientation would set doctrines against each other: mechanism and vitalism, continuist geneticism and the theory of sudden mutations, quantum theories and corpuscular ideas taken separately, social 'institutions' and 'structures' separated from 'processes', or movement, of experienced spontaneity, formalism and historicism isolated from each other in sociology, and so on. Here again, dialectical hyper-empiricism would be an appeal to the continual upsetting of 'systems' in favour of constantly renewed in-depth study of the problems.

In order to play its role therefore, this orientation cannot link its fate with any particular philosophical or scientific position, for all science and philosophy must go through this severe trial, the 'ordeal', the purificatory fire of dialectical hyper-empiricism as a starting point . . .

Extract from 'L'hyper-empirisme dialectique, ses applications en sociologie', in *Cahiers Internationaux de Sociologie*, XV, 1953.

2. THE DIALECTIC BETWEEN SOCIOLOGY AND HISTORY

Historical reality, which some writers still refer to as 'historicity', is a privileged sector of social reality, i.e. the constantly changing total social phenomena, as well as the structures, works and circumstances through which they are expressed. It is characterized by collective and individual consciousness of human liberty whose concentrated action may succeed in upsetting or modifying the structures and, to a certain extent, may permit rebellion against tradition. *Historical reality is therefore only the Promethean part of social reality*; it is contrasted with the other part of this reality which is not so or which is so only to a very small degree, as in the case of 'archaic' societies and, with some exceptions, patriarchal or traditional societies. The historical reality coinciding with this sector of social reality where men taken collectively and individually consider the possibility of the transformation or the upheaval of social structures as a consequence of concentrated human action, is exemplified by any total social phenomenon of a global nature where there is consciousness of possible revolution or counter-revolution, resulting from the will of the participants. I do not need to emphasise the fact that the degrees of the Prometheanism or the historical character of a social reality are many and that it is incumbent on the sociologist to establish a scale correlating them with various types of social frameworks.

This 'historical reality' is studied both by the science of history

and sociology. But, whilst historiography or historical knowledge concentrates exclusively on it, sociology seeks to compare
it with non-historical or only slightly historical social frameworks
and consequently aims to place it in broader social ensembles
where microsocial and group elements that are only to a certain
extent penetrated by 'historicity' also appear. Already one senses
here a possible primary tension between the science of history
and sociology; for, if the former overemphasises the primacy of
global societies 'making history', the latter is too preoccupied
with showing the complex relationship between the social scales
which presuppose each other.

There is another tension in addition to this first one, which
can only be resolved by the empirico-realist dialectic. If historians
tend towards an over-intense unification of social reality, even
though the Promethean manifestations of this reality in fact lend
themselves to unification less well than others, sociologists reveal
the opposite tendency. They are tempted to give in to an over-
developed differentiation and diversification of the competing
social frameworks even though, in certain sectors of the field
that they are studying, unification finds less resistance than in
historical reality. This paradoxical situation, which leads to
dialectical complementarity between sociology and history, is reinforced by the contrast between the methods and conceptualizations of the two sciences and, certainly, by the contrast between
the objects of knowledge constructed by each of them.

Sociology has as its method the typology of total social phenomena, their structures, and the cultural works which cement
the structures. Without challenging the typology, the science of
history by-passes it in seeking out the unrepeatable and the
irreplaceable in the turning points of the development of Promethean societies. It thus singularizes global structures and
circumstances to an extreme and, even more, the total social
phenomena which are subjacent and overflow into them. *It
emphasizes the continuity of passage between structures, the
continuity of their excesses, even the continuity of their ruptures,*

and the continuity of unrepeatable chains. On the other hand, sociology emphasizes the discontinuity of types as well as the discontinuity of structures and total social phenomena, within each scale, as well as in the relationships between these scales. From the viewpoint of method, history as science is led to fill in the breaks, to build bridges between the various structures, between these and the total social phenomena, and between the total social phenomena themselves. *Historical method is, therefore, much more continuist than sociological method.* This caused a historian as conscious of method as Fernand Braudel to say that he would like to 'restore the pure unitary light which is essential to it'.[2] Only he forgets that this light is to be found only in the science of historians and not in historical reality. Now, this is precisely one of the aspects of the dialectic which is at stake between history and sociology, a dialectic whose terms I shall soon try to specify.

The continuism of the historical method is confirmed by the singular and closed nature of 'historical causality'. In sociological explanation, causality is not the only process of explanation and does not always succeed. Furthermore, sociological causality, which is already singular, never goes to the extreme of this singularity, but involves various degrees. 'Historical causality', on the contrary, intensifies the singularity of the causal link even more than sociological causality does, while making the relationships between causes and effects closer, more continuous and consequently even more certain. In fact, in time that has already past, but has been reconstructed and made present, the time to which 'historical knowledge' refers, the causal chain, while asserting itself as strictly unrepeatable and irreplaceable, so contracts and becomes so continuous that the historian arrives at much more rigorous and much more satisfying explanations than those that the sociologist might offer.

Surely this is the reason for the somewhat exaggerated belief

[2] Cf. F. Braudel, Histoire et sociologie, in *Traité de sociologie*, 1958, tome I, *op. cit.*, p. 96.

of some historians in the strength of historical determinism? One meets it in Marx,[3] but it is mainly official Marxism which dressed it in exaggerated terms such as the 'implacable turning of the wheel of history'. This belief, which is fairly widespread among certain contemporary historians who fancy themselves as sociologists, is found even in Sartre who suggests reconciling liberty and necessity through 'historical reason'. To avoid the temptation of historicist dogmatism, an appeal to the dialectic between sociology and historical sciences is necessary at this point, by revealing the complementarity and mutual involvement between historical explanation and sociological explanation.

The same can be said of the relationship between sociological time and historical time,[4] the multiplicity of which is revealed by the two sciences, but they appear in different aspects and raise the problem of their unification in a particular way. Sociology mainly emphasizes the discontinuity of various social times as well as the relativity of their unification. History as a science, on the other hand, gives such importance to the continuity of various times that unification threatens to dissolve the multiplicity of these times. This divergence is due to the difference in methods of these two sciences.

In historical reality, the multiplicity of social time is accentuated by its relationship with Promethianism. This latter favours time of irregular pulsations, time in advance of itself, and creative time, though they are seriously limited by time of long

---

[3] This is so even though Marx recognized that *'men make their own history'*; but, he added, they *'do not always know that they are making it'*. This sentence calls for dual distinctions: (a) if they are more or less conscious in historical or promethean societies, they are never so in 'archaic' societies; (b) with regard to historical or promethean societies, Marx is too pessimistic in attributing the power to make history consciously only to the proletarian class, whose class consciousness is confused with its doctrine.

[4] Cf. on this subject my duplicated course *La multiplicité des temps sociaux* (Paris, CDU, 1958, *passim*) and particularly pp. 35–9, 129, which contain my response to F. Braudel's criticisms. Cf. also my article 'Structures sociales et multiplicité des temps', in *Bulletin de la Société française de Philosophie*, 52nd year, meeting of 31st January, 1959, pp. 99–142.

duration and slowed down.[5] However, in the science of history ('historiography' or 'historical knowledge'), these real historical times *are reconstructed according to the ideological point of view of the historian, who is tempted to choose certain times to the detriment of others.*

This is because the times studied by the science of history and which are past, are reconstructed by the latter according to the criteria of the societies, classes and groups contemporary to the historians. Thus societies are constantly being pushed into re-writing their history, making past time both present and ideological. The multiplicity of time that faces the historian, as well as their exaggerated unification, is not so much that of historical reality, as the multiplicity of various reconstructions of time past, and their re-established and reinforced unities.

This second multiplicity and unification—which is inevitable here—can be reduced to various interpretations about the continuity of time. The competition between this dual multiplicity and unification of 'historical times' becomes so much more dramatic that the historians belonging to the different societies, classes or groups succeed in reviving past time only at the expense of the projection of their 'present' into the 'past' that they are studying. Now they cannot arrive at this projection without presupposing a continuity and a unity between the different scales of time appropriate to different societies. This is why *'the great temptation to which the science of history is prey is the 'prediction of the past' which often turns into the projection of this prediction into the future'* . . . Here a dialectic appears in the very heart of historical knowledge, a dialectic which manifests its full scope in the complex relationships between history and sociology.

[5] Cf. the article on 'La longue durée' by F. Braudel, in *Annales*, 1958, No. 4, pp. 725–53, which questions me, particularly in pages 750–1, without taking account of my more recent analyses: *La multiplicité des temps sociaux*, 1958, pp. 35–9, 139 (duplicated course), and 'Structures sociales et multiplicité des temps', in *Bulletin de la Société française de Philosophie*, 1959, pp. 99–142. In the following pages the reader will, I hope, find a response to F. Braudel's criticisms.

In short, one can and one must speak of *the ambiguity of historical time*, as well as the ambiguity of its multiplicity and its intensified unification: (a) ambiguity in the discrepancy between times of historical reality and times which are projected by historians; (b) ambiguity in the tension between the dual multiplicity and the dual unification of historical times: real multiplicity and unification on the one hand; interpreted multiplicity and unification on the other; (c) ambiguity in the competition of their multiplicities, both real and projected, and their projected rather than real continuist unifications; (d) ambiguity in the rigorous singularization of historical times which merely serves to reinforce their constructed continuities; (e) ambiguity in the fact that past, completed time maintains few traits in common with *time in process of making itself*.

How is one to study the vicissitudes of historical time, its multiplicity and its exaggerated unity, without having recourse to the process of *dialectical ambiguity*? Now, these ambiguities are aggravated, at certain points by *antinomies* which also require enlightenment by the process of dialectical polarization.

Extract from *Dialectique et Sociologie*, Paris, Flammarion, 1962

3. DEPTH SOCIOLOGY

Contemporary sociology is in the process of being transformed into a science whose first step is the study of the social reality in depth. If the sociology of the 19th century can be characterized as uni-dimensional, 20th century sociology is above all *pluri-dimensional*. It is a depth sociology. Social reality appears to the experienced eye of the sociologist to be arranged in steps, levels, tiered planes, in increasingly deep layers. These steps and stages interpenetrate and permeate each other. However, they are continually in conflict: their relationships are tense, antinomic, dialectical. There are inextricable tensions inherent in all social reality that one might describe as vertical tensions. Horizontal conflicts and tensions occur in addition to these polarisations and related implications at each depth level; group struggle —particularly class antagonism—is an example. The task of sociology consists of discovering all these tensions and conflicts, by placing them in their specific social context, for their acuity varies with the multiplicity of types of structures and sometimes even of circumstances. It is no more the task of sociology to resolve than to camouflage these conflicts. The vocation of the sociologist is first of all to recognize his capacity for uncovering these antimonies and latent tensions in a particular social reality, seen as a 'total social phenomenon'. The intellectual honesty of the sociological researcher is measured by the strength which he displays in his constant struggle against temptations to conceal or silence the bitter drama which, at any moment in the existence of a society, is taking place between their different stages and levels.

The pluri-dimensional character of the social reality, which is manifested in the various depth levels has been experienced by many thinkers from very different schools of thought. To quote only the most important of them, Proudhon and Marx, Durkheim and Hauriou, Bergson and the phenomenologists (proceeding through inversion and reduction towards the immediate) strove whether deliberately or not to reveal stages within social reality. We cannot now spend time analysing any of these antecedents. We can only mention the distinction that Proudhon[6] established between 'collective forces' and 'collective reason' and their intermediary, 'law'. 'Material productive forces', 'social structure' or 'relationships of production', 'real consciousness, both social and individual', and its products (language, law, knowledge, arts, etc.), and lastly 'ideological superstructure', in the early writings of Marx.[7] The 'morphological' or material

[6] Cf. my discussion in the *Idée du droit social*, 1932, pp. 348 and ff. and in my duplicated course, 1955, facs. II.

[7] Cf. 'La sociologie de Karl Marx', Vol II of *La vocation*, and *Dialectique et sociologie, op. cit.*, pp. 125–32.

'basis', 'institutions' (or 'pre-established ways of doing things') referring directly to organizations, rites and practices, symbols, values, collective ideas and ideals (both products and producers of social reality), and lastly the 'free currents' of collective consciousness in Durkheim.[8] The organized, hardened, cold superstructure ('the mechanical as a veneer on the living'), the ceremonial side (rites, practices, models and symbols included)— 'ceremonies being to the social body what clothes are to the individual body' and representing the 'ready-to-wear' in 'living society'—and finally 'social spontaneity' which is 'always in turmoil', the 'igneous material' of society, source of 'social mobility' and 'volcanic eruptions' all appeared in Bergson at the time of the *Rire*.[9] The five acts of the 'drama of personification' of 'objective institutions'—unity for external usage, organization for internal usage, organization democratized through its root in the 'underlying founding union', spontaneous institution 'having a common work to accomplish', and remaining as the psychic and spiritual infrastructure of any group, and lastly 'objective and eternal idea' perceived collectively and being incarnated in the institution-group appear in Maurice Hauriou's work.[10] All these attempts at distinguishing levels seem to me not only very incomplete but laden with philosophical reservations and compromised by a lack of relativism, and, consequently, antidogmatism, which in the end, are alone capable of transforming sociology into a science.

Extract from *La vocation actuelle de la sociologie*, Vol. I: *Vers la sociologie differentielle*, 1st edn., Paris, Presses Universitaires de France, 1950.

[8] Cf. Vol. II, chap. VIII.
[9] Cf. Vol. II, chap. XII.
[10] Cf. my discussion in *Idée du droit social, op. cit.*, pp. 684–95.

4. THE PROBLEM OF EXPLANATION

What are the reasons for the patent failure of sociology in recent years, or even the last half-century, in the realm of explanation? As I have already mentioned, the reasons are various.

First it is related to the general crisis of rigid deterministic statements. Determinism has been pushed too much towards necessity which no longer feeds on reality. Determinism—which is integration of facts into one of the many concrete (experienced, known, constructed) real or universal frameworks which always remain contingent and whose coherence and continuity exist to varying degrees—has not been sufficiently distinguished from the different technical processes of observing this determinism. There exists a plurality of determinisms and a multiplicity of techniques permitting them to be observed. As neither causal laws, functional laws nor laws of evolution are applicable to the social frameworks, given their dynamism, their inconsistency and the wealth of meanings attributed to them, it was thought it might be possible to restrict oneself to statistical laws which explain nothing, being content with calculations of probabilities, which are not applicable to all aspects of social reality. What has been forgotten are the functional correlations, the tendential regularities, and—first and foremost—singular causality, which is the technical process of determinist explanation having the widest application in sociology.[11]

Secondly, there is abuse of the opposition between understanding and explanation. There has been a great deal of benefit gained in France and the United States, from the 'understanding of the internal meaning of behaviour' of which Max Weber made himself the champion, mainly in order to get away from explanation in sociology. Nevertheless, it has not been realized that, for Weber himself, it was first of all necessary to understand

---

[11] Cf. my analyses in *Déterminismes sociaux et liberté humaine*, 1955, pp. 15–67, and *passim*.

(*deutend Verstehen*), in order to explain later, and this through recourse to causality. Still less has attention been paid to the fact that Weber was not the inventor of *verstehen*; that he took it from Dilthey and changed the meaning; that Weber found himself in a very awkward position on the subject of understanding. Dilthey was preoccupied with the perception of real totalities, characterizing the social and historical world. He considered that all explanation was necessarily mechanistic and because of that even destroyed the totalities, the wholes. For him, understanding and explanation as alternatives could be reduced to that of the whole and the sum of its parts, the sociocultural ensemble, and atomism. Dilthey did not see the dialectic which is established between understanding and explaining, for he did not see that all explanation, even a mechanistic one (which is certainly not the only form of explanation), presupposes a real ensemble into which the act is integrated. Explanation is impossible without understanding of the ensemble. In short, he did not see that one can not explain without understanding, or understand without explaining, and that it is a question of inseparable moments of the same process, where the emphasis varies according to the character of the totality under examination. Also he did not realize that the human sciences, particularly sociology and history, are distinct from the natural sciences only because of a very great wealth of human significance attached to the totalities that they study. This makes understanding more prominent in this field without separating it from explanation. As for Weber, the supporter of the closed, inwardlooking consciousness, and an intransigent nominalist, he made concrete totalities disappear and denied perception because it could only be intuitive. Calvinism and Kantianism were combined in his thinking, and understanding was reduced to introspection about 'internal meanings' which, in the best of cases, were merely 'reflections' of ideal values and ideas, being outside reality, including social reality . . . Thus, through a degraded 'understanding' and the barely concealed spiritualism of meanings, sociology was subjected to systematizations from theology, philosophy and the independent social sciences. The need for explanation following understanding disappeared for want of a real social framework, which Weber served only to demolish and destroy. Who could be surprised in these conditions at the crop of rare explanations that he put forward, for example, that the capitalist régime is explained by the calvinist dogma of predestination and is confirmed in economic success . . .

Thirdly, the regression and lack of explanation in sociology are due to the tendency of each particular branch of sociology (whose number has multiplied) to be enclosed within its own limits as far as explanation is concerned. If one can justify, to a certain point, sectors of the 'sociology of the mind' (sociology of knowledge, sociology of morals, sociology of religion, sociology of law, sociology of education, etc.) when they take special precautions in the realm of explanation to avoid losing or dissolving the very field of their research, one should also remember that by asserting themselves as branches of sociology (and not as independent human sciences or as philosophical disciplines) they can only be distinguished from each other at the point of *departure* and not the point of *arrival*. They can begin with any depth level or any specific collective activity. But to finish up with an overall view that reveals the total social phenomena at work and the total men who participate in them and who do not allow themselves to be cut into pieces, they must take account of all the depth levels, all the scales (manifestations of sociability, groups, classes, global societies) and all the connections and disjunctions, including those which occur between organizations, structures and astructural elements, as well as between acts and works. The discontinuous, dynamic types that sociology establishes in all its branches and which culminate in the types of global total social phenomena are developed not in order to establish *images d'Epinal*, but to promote *explanation* in sociology. These types are neither 'phenotypes' nor 'genotypes' (K. Lewin), but designations of real frameworks in which

specific volcanic forces rumble and where changes and explosions
are produced . . .

Fourthly, the lack of enthusiasm for explanation in sociology,
or in a word, the crisis of explanation, comes from the failure of
dialectical processes in sociology. In non-Marxist sociology, this
failure is due to the desire to compartmentalize and the lack of
any dialectical analysis, which is necessary for the concrete perception of the total social phenomena in action. In Marxist sociology it comes from a dogmatic interpretation of the dialectic that
is subject to a preconceived materialism, and from the confusion
between dialectical analysis and explanation, which in reality
are always separate.

Extracts from 'La crise de l'explication en sociologie' in *Cah.
inter. de socio.*, XXI, 1956.

5. SOCIAL DETERMINISMS

If one is freed from preconceptions and confusions, one must
recognize that the only presupposition implied by determinism
as such, is the statement that there exist real ensembles or frameworks, or, more broadly, real and concrete universes, and that
one can attribute to them a certain coherence, which varies in
degree. Yet this coherence is never univocal. In fact, it is always
characterized by its position as intermediary between opposites
that would be wrongly hypostatized as contradictory.[12] It is a
question of terms which are only fully grasped in the light of
the complementarity of compensation: such as the continuous
and the discontinuous, the quantitative and the qualitative, the
heterogeneous and the homogeneous, duration and the moment,
the reversible and the irreversible and, most particularly, the
coherent and the contingent. This complementarity of compen-

---

[12] This is what Bergson did in *Les données immédiates de la conscience* and
which led him to a hopeless dualism, abandoned in *Matière et mémoire* and
L'évolution créatrice.

sation opens up the way to almost infinite degrees of intermediary paths which end up being indispensable to their very
rejectors (who are concerned with hardening opposites into conceptual alternatives which would be mutually exclusive, and
thus with pushing totally contradictory antimonies towards extreme cases—which are, in fact, inextricably linked not only in
experienced reality, but in the reality as conceived by different
sciences). However—beyond the exceptions constituted by being
and non-being, absolute necessity and unlimited creative freedom,
the contradiction of which is either spotlighted or resolved according to the philosophical position adopted—by polarising opposites, one merely ends up *inflating antimonies,* and one falls
into their *fetishism,* if one is not aware that this is just one
of the many dialectical processes of illumination: polarisation
(which is only rarely necessary and does not exclude other processes, such as complementarity, mutual dialectical involvement,
reciprocity of perspectives and so on). It is only due to the
infinite degrees of transition and compromise between complementary or mutually involved opposites that reality can be
presented to us in the multiformity of its frameworks and its
manifestations, and that various determinisms can be attributed
to them.

Thus, all reality and all determinism which might control it
are plunged into the environment of 'discontinuous continuity'
or 'continuous discontinuity', 'qualitative-quantitative' or
'quantitative-qualitative' (quantity itself appearing in the form
of degrees between the extensive and the intensive), 'heterogeneous homogeneity' and 'homogeneous heterogeneity', 'duration' cut through by the moment, and the moment, or rather
moments, inherent in duration, 'stable change' and 'changing
stability', in a word: contingency making concessions to coherence and coherence making compromises with the fortuitous.
Coherent contingency and *contingent coherence,* are the primor-
dial characteristics of all determinism and reality. It is not
surprising that recourse to the process of dialectical hyper-

G

empiricism[13] is necessary in order to appreciate the problem. Gaston Bachelard felt this in his *Dialectique de la durée*, which is also the dialectic of the moment, and which is devoted to criticism of the dualist and continuist tendency in Bergson's thought. But he does not entirely do justice either to Bergson's latent discontinuism, or the multiplicity of pathways between the coherent and contingent.[14]

All determinism, inasmuch as it feeds on reality, is effected in time and usually in extension, if not in space, or, to the extent that one asserts that the two cannot be separated, in space-time or time-space (Einstein). What concerns me is the statement that the time of determinism bears no relation to eternity, either as an antimony to it, or as transition towards it, that it is a matter of the immanent participation by stages in 'living eternity' (Plotin, and in another form, Hegel), or of a stable hierarchy between *eternitas, aevum* and *tempus* of scholastic philosophy. The temporalist realism implied in determinism leads to the recognition of a *multiplicity of competing times*, which are in the same position of intermediaries between complementary opposites as the determinisms and realities controlled by them. There will be as many temporalities[15] as determinisms, the plurality of both being a function of the diversity of the real frameworks or concrete universes which engender them through their movement, and then themselves pass away.

The clarification of the concept of determinism could have found a basis in the direction indicated by Bergson: he opened the way to a theory of the muliplicity of time and to a temporalist realism, by contrasting the qualitative and the quanti-

[13] Cf. my study in *Cahiers internationaux de Sociologie*, 1953, Vol. XV.

[14] Cf. *La dialectique de la durée*, 1936, 2nd ed., 1950 and by the same author, *L'intuition de l'instant*, 1933, pp. 10–11.

[15] Cf. for the history of the theories of time, Jean Wahl, *Traité de métaphysique*, 1953, pp. 219–27 and 285–308, who studied them in two different categories, relating one to quantity and the other to quality. But he doubts the possibility of this separation, as well as the validity of the isolation of time from what happens within it. Surely this is tantamount to recognizing the reality of a multiplicy of times?

tative in time and later finding himself driven to talking about 'different densities of duration'. But Bergson himself foreclosed this path, by restricting his discovery to the opposition between two times: qualitative duration experienced by the inner self and spatialized time of science, the former being immeasurable, the latter not being an irreversible succession. Although in *Matière et mémoire* and *L'évolution créatrice*, he freed qualitative time from its link with the subjective idealism of the inner self, and although he discovered 'concrete extension' more qualitative than conceptualized space, and although he placed matter, life, the psychic and the social in different degrees of qualitative time, he did not succeed in liberating these degrees from phases of 'de-spatialisation'. He could not rid himself of the identification of conceptualizations of time and concrete extensions with their qualification and spatialization. He did not realize that the 'construct' of the sciences, including their conceptualized temporalities, could be based on the experience of these latter. Finally he remained faithful to a monism and a continuism that was primarily vitalist and secondly spiritualist. Thus, in his last work, after realizing his failure to draw out all the consequences from his realist temporalism—which proposed to dethrone eternity, including living eternity—he tried to reconcile time and eternity, supported by the Plotinian doctrine of reminiscence.

Extract from *Déterminismes sociaux et liberté humaine*, Paris, Presses Universitaires de France, 1955.

6 THE CONCEPT OF SOCIAL STRUCTURE

If I have dwelt on certain deficiencies in sociological theory, for which the concept of social structure sometimes serves only as a screen and as a damper, as it were, even for a scholar of the stature of Radcliffe-Brown, it is because I am convinced that, despite the many abuses of this term, it does correspond to real needs in present-day sociological analysis. Some of these legitimate needs can be deciphered from the way in which Radcliffe-Brown himself poses the problem. I shall begin with these in order to reveal several others later on.

(A) First is the sometimes unconscious need to get rid of the 'sociologies of order' and the 'sociologies of progress', as well as their unfruitful synthesis along the lines of Auguste Comte. Social structures cannot in any way be reduced either to order or progress, both terms implying scarcely camouflaged value judgements and which, from the sociological point of view, merely serve to dogmatize divergent and, in the majority of cases, opposite points of view, which arise in each particular social structure. One of the specific vocations of any social structure (partial or global) consists precisely of looking for a certain balance between its points of view, by using multiple hierarchies. These never remain static, given their complexity and their very precariousness: they are continually structured, destructured and restructured, or else they explode to give way to a new structure.

(B) Second, the concept of social structure corresponds to the profound need to break the false division between 'static' and 'dynamic' sociology. This division has done incalculable harm to sociology. The social structure is a permanent process: it is involved in a movement of perpetual destructuration and re-structuration, being one aspect of *society in action*, which, as a 'work' can not exist for a moment without the intervention of the 'act', a continually renewed attempt at unification and orientation.

Social structures can even sometimes prove to be more dynamic than the astructural or non-structural elements of the total social phenomena. It is a question of fact, situation, conjuncture. But even when, as normally, they are more stable and less explosive, they still move, and their rhythm depends on the scale of multiple temporalities which characterizes them and is appropriate to them. For 'slowed down time', 'deceptive time' or 'surprise time', 'time of irregular pulsations between the appearance and disappearance of rhythms', 'cyclical time' of 'dancing on the spot', 'retarding time', 'time of alternation between fast and slow', 'time in advance of itself' and 'explosive time of creation'[16] are in different degrees of virtuality and actuality, always present in all social structures, in hierarchy, in combination, in interpenetration, in collision in different ways. The 'duration' of a social structure is therefore never a 'response' but a *battle*, a procession through tortuous routes opened up by the *multiplicity of social time . . .*

Thus, the opposition between social statics and dynamics is to be rejected not only because it hides the astructural, spontaneous, effervescent elements of social life, and the ' total social phenomena', the most complete volcanic manifestations of 'society in action' when it is, as it were, laid bear, but also, and especially because it prevents understanding what a 'social structure' is, with its various rhythms of structuration, destructuration, restructuration, and total upheaval of structures.

Even in the so-called 'exact' sciences, or natural sciences, not only in biology and physiology (which deal with life), but also in contemporary physics and chemistry, the separation of the static from the dynamic seems increasingly difficult, as revealed by quantum ideas of light, the general theory of relativity, physico-chemistry, etc., where the dialectic of relationships and transformations continually gains ground over the Aristotelianism which imprisoned Auguste Comte.

(C) Third, the concept of social structure is currently the centre of attention for sociologists and ethnologists because it helps them to transcend what has sometimes been called 'culturalism', that is to say, the mummification of civilizations into entities that were intended to be studied 'in themselves',[17]

---

[16] Cf. on the different temporalities, my *Déterminismes, op. cit.*, pp. 38–40 and *passim*, and Chap. XIII on 'a multiplicité des temps sociaux' in vol. II of *La vocation.*

[17] This is why C. Lévi-Strauss, when he refers to Ruth Benedict, author of *Patterns of Culture*, 1934, for polemical reasons as a 'structuralist' (*Anthropologie structurale*, 1958, p. 353), compromises the whole movement or . . . is counting on the ignorance of his readers.

independently of the societies and groups which produce them or use them as beneficiaries. It is well known that different global societies can participate in the same civilization and that the cultural works of certain civilizations can be revived and reinterpreted in various social structures and at different periods of history. But to conclude from that, either that civilizations are like the parts of an orchestra where the life and the arrangement of societies into structures develop, is to fall into what Radcliffe-Briwn quite rightly characterized as a 'fantastic reification of abstractions', under which there is usually camouflaged a dogmatic spiritualism, recognized or not.

The problem of the relationship between civilization and society finds a satisfying solution in the concept of social structures for which cultural works and systems act as the framework. They cement their many balances, precarious and relative as they always are, through the signs, signals, symbols, ideas and values appropriate to them. In fact, the social structures are revealed in a concrete way both as producers and products of cultural works. Civilizations can be autochthonal or, partially at least, derived or transmitted; but they are real and efficacious only through their cementing role, fortifying the precarious balances which constitute a social structure: even when the social structure only participates in a civilization as a beneficiary, it adapts the civilization to its needs and in this way, transforms it and even partially recreates it.

These three primary reasons for the attraction exercised by the concept of social structure on contemporary sociology and ethnology are implicit in the work of Radcliffe-Brown and his school; they are more or less easily deciphered. By contrast, the reasons that I shall discuss next are much less clear, especially at first glance.

(D) Fourth, the concept of social structure responds to the quest for whatever it is that makes 'organisations' possible, without being confused with them and without being equated with the spontaneous, fluid, diffuse elements of the social reality. *There is no sense in talking of social structure except when one is able to make a clear distinction between the social structure and the organization or organizations* which might constitute one element entering into the balances of the structure, or an inadequate expression of the structure, but this is never the same thing.

From this point of view, it is particularly appropriate to point out the confusion existing in Anglo-Saxon, especially American, literature, where so many books are devoted to the problem of *social organization* but where the precise meaning of the term is lost. In fact, as I have already mentioned, one often speaks of *informal organization* to designate not only unorganized elements, but even non-structured and non-structurable ('astructural' in my terminology) elements of social reality. Similarly, the authors who devote their works to the problems of 'social structure' (e.g. Murdock, Parsons, Marion Levy Jr., etc.) pay no attention to the difference existing between structure and organization, and take pleasure in using these two terms with the most hopeless *promiscuity* ...

It is pointless to emphasize earlier mistakes (outside the concept of structure) that equate groups and organizations such as the primary Durkheimian notion characterizing social reality by constraint (which, properly speaking, can only be imposed by organizations), or the formalist interpretations of Simmel, von Wiese, MacIver, Hiller and others, who saw no means of arriving at the unification of relationships in an ensemble without the intervention of an organization (their nominalism prevented them both from grasping any idea of totality or concept of structure). I have discussed many times in this book the necessity for getting rid of these aberrations by emphasising the fact that organizations constitute only one level, one stage of social reality, and that groups and global societies, even when they are fully organized, even 'over-organised', are never completely expressed in organizations, and are still less to be equated with them. This is as true for the spontaneous strata of groups and societies, their astructural elements, their 'setting in motion' as 'total social phenomena', as for the social structures—which are infinitely more vast, more rich and more complex sectors and aspects of social reality. The rigidity and distance of an organization manifest various degrees which depend not only on the technique of their management and the measure to which they are open to penetration from the 'total social phenomenon'—the centre which presides over their birth, their functioning, the constitution of their schemes, their persistence or their upheaval—but also from the partial or global social structures in which they participate. In fact, the importance, efficacy, role, characteristics, weight and number of organizations vary as a function of the social structures which make them possible and into which they are integrated.

Not only can a group or a global society be strongly structured without being organized or even expressible in a single organization (for example: social classes, nations, and international societies), but also the partial or global social structures slot in between spontaneous social life and organizations, by playing the role of *tertium gaudens*, 'third party'. The social structures benefit from all the other elements, sometimes succumbing to this complex game. Far from playing the role of mediators or intermediaries, or still less as synthesists, between the opposites, they struggle with these elements, but never succeed in completely mastering them, given the fact that they themselves merely overlap and express only very partially the 'total social phenomena'.

This results in the particularly tense, complex, eventful, precarious, character of any social structure, its exaggerated intestinal conflicts, its perpetual course towards renewed structuration or destruction, or even explosion, its appeal to ever necessary collective efforts, the impossibility of detaching the structure as 'work' from the 'society in action' . . .

(E) Fifth, the concept of social structure exercises the same attractions in sociology and ethnology as *Gestaltism* in psychology. The social structures are *configurations*, and *ambiances*, *ensembles* that are *in motion, prominent* and *concretised;* configurations, ambiances, concrete and mobile cohesions which provide empirical data for the thesis that in sociology the whole is irreducible to its constituent, participant elements, but cannot at the same time exist without them, the two moving together. Being in no way identical to the total social phenomena, even when real collective units are concerned (i.e. macrosociological units: global groups and units), when these units are structured the social structures provide the closest, most convenient, most accessible reflections of them.

Just as the purpose of the concept of *Gestalt* in psychology is to make clear that a perception actually or virtually precedes scattered perceptions, *a fortiori* separate sensations which are only secondary and minor elements of it, the concept of social structure tries to highlight the fact that the social ensemble, complex though it may be, virtually or actually precedes all the balances, hierarchies and scales, those of groups and classes, manifestations of sociability, depth levels, modes of division of labour and money, social regulations, models, signs, signals, symbols, ideas and values, temporalities, and determinisms. On the other hand, it is precisely the precarious balance of all these elements which characterizes a social structure. Therefore there is a striking affinity between Gestaltism in psychology and *structuralism* in sociology. Who could be surprised at this relationship? It is sufficient to note that the 'total social phenomena' and the 'total psychic phenomena' in part overlap and that the *Gestalt* in psychology and the *structure* in sociology play the same role as substitutes, *intermediaries*, which provide data for concrete empirical research in the rather inaccessible area of *totalities in motion*.

Social structures are intermediary between totalities and their expressions in social regulations, their manifestations in what used to be called 'institutions', as well as their externalization in organized apparatus. They are intermediary between the

H

'total social phenomenon' and the various human significances which are grafted on to it. They are intermediary between 'motion' and a particular stabilization, and intermediary *between the existence of a total social phenomenon and the way it is seen and represented* . . .

(F) When one intends to study *types of global societies*[18] (to be distinguished from microsociological types, or types of sociability, and types of particular groups), the establishment of this typology, as I have already suggested, is possible only by starting with their structures. In fact, unlike particular groups (omitting manifestations of sociability, which are astructural), every global society *without exception* possesses a structure and the study of this is the only means of constructing the types of global total social phenomena. I have gone as far as to say, in *Déterminismes sociaux et liberté humaine*, that global societies and global social structures are the same thing. That is incorrect, for the two manifestations can be either ahead of or behind each other. Furthermore, a *concrete* global society is much richer than its structure, however complex it may be, which is but one aspect, one sector, one very partial expression of the total social phenomenon. But, in order to grasp the total global social pheno-menon in all its fullness, I have found no other solution than to start with a constructed type, which can only be a particular type of global social structure. I think therefore that whoever intends to study a global society from the sociological point of view must begin by studying its type, and whoever wants to study a global type must necessarily begin with its social struc-ture, which lends itself to a similar typology (the type always being half-way between generalization and individualization).

(G) The seventh and last reason justifying the contemporary importance of the concept of social structure for sociological and ethnological thought consists of the need to distinguish between *social structure* and *social conjuncture*.

[18] Cf. for the definition of the concept of global society, *Déterminismes, op. cit.*, pp. 193 ff.

The development of an autonomous, particular social science, political economy, has given value to the concept of conjuncture. The succession of situations of crisis and prosperity, without a change in the economic régime is a patent fact, especially in the framework of capitalism. This fact quickly attracted the attention of political economists of all leanings. This science—insofar as it keeps autonomy in relation to sociology—is in fact an eminently practical, applied discipline, which seeks to schematize the best means of obtaining maximum prosperity and productivity in a given social structure. It cannot therefore avoid observing fluctuations of prices, over-production and under-production, and the purchasing power of money.

The founders of 'economic sociology', to give it its proper name, from Marx to Simiand, have broadened the problem by seeking out the social causes of economic crises, and 'fluctuations of long and short duration' under capitalist régimes. It is in this way that the concept of 'economic conjecture' became the economists' centre of attention and ended up by being integrated into the wider, more delicate problem of 'social conjecture' as a whole.

Now, social conjunctures, whether they are stable or turbulent, favourable or unfavourable to a certain social class, or even to a certain functional group, or manifestation of sociability or interpretation of cultural works, or political, religious, philosophical, scientific orientation, etc., or to a certain persuasion in the collective mentality, most often fluctuate without the social structures where these conjunctures arise undergoing changes. However, the relationship between structure and conjuncture is much more complex than it seems at first sight. In fact, there are conjunctures which may promote the destructuration and even the overthrow of the structures (did not the socio-economic conjuncture at the end of the 18th century promote the French Revolution?); other conjunctures lead to strengthened structuration or restructuration; and, certain conjunctures, and these are the most common, do not touch the structure directly or, in any case, in a perceptible way.

Inversely, social structures always make their mark on conjunctures, which are possible only within their framework, and it is sometimes the structures which directly provoke the conjunctures, either unconsciously by struggling for maintenance of their many, precarious balances, or consciously through 'political, administrative, economic or demographic measures' which have foreseen or unforeseen consequences.

Extract from *La vocation actuelle de la sociologie*, Vol. I: *Vers la sociologie différentielle*, Paris, Presses Universitaires de France, 1950, 4th edn., 1968.

IV. THE THEORY OF PRAXIS

1. PLURALISM AND SOCIAL LAW

From the description of present day social reality, it is clear that new resistance to the realization of democratic values requires totally new techniques for achieving human liberty. These techniques are linked to the pluralist theory, which is increasingly more vigorously applied, and is combined with a juridical symbolism which takes account of the liberty, dignity and autonomy of ensembles, groups and individuals.

However, pluralist theory has several clearly distinct meanings. To avoid all confusion, it is necessary to specify them.

From the sociological point of view, pluralism is an observable *fact* in every society without exception. Every society is always a microcosm of particular groups, limited, in conflict, in balance, in combination, integrated and arranged hierarchically in the global ensemble, a microcosm allowing many various combinations, conditioned by historical situations. The web of social life is therefore characterized by a fundamental factual pluralism, the tension between groups and their moving balances, constituting the fundamental social material. The extent of the multiplicity, role, intensity of autonomy, value and strength of particular groups in a type of given society, may vary, they may increase or diminish, but they never disappear. This social pluralism may serve to the good or the detriment, domination or emancipation, liberty or servitude, autocracy or democracy. At the present time it is seen both in economic feudalism and employers' domination in factories, in the class struggle and the tendencies towards disintegration of global societies, and in the development of professional syndicalism, workers' rights, co-operatives, and institutions attempting to balance the rights of producers and consumers.[1]

Pluralism as an ideal is clearly contrasted with this actual pluralism *de fait*. It concerns a moral, juridical ideal, consisting of a harmony between variety and unity, mutually engendering an equilibrium between personal values and group values, a reciprocal immanence between the wholes and their many parts. Pluralism as an ideal, inasmuch as it is not directed towards a total dispersion into the many, or does not degenerate into an anarchic singularism, is not entirely pluralist. It integrates the pluralist variety and equivalence (which are an essential manifestation of human liberty) into a wider synthesis which alone gives a criterion of selection among the many. If one examines carefully the democratic ideal, by going into its historical and symbolic expressions to get to its living spirit, it must seem obvious that democracy is based on the principle of equivalence between personal values and group values, a principle realized through variety in unity, that is to say, that the democratic ideal has its source in the pluralist ideal. The synthesis through which the democratic ideal is expressed, emphasizes 'variety' based on 'liberty', 'unity' based on the 'equality' of the people and the groups participating in the fraternal community. Going further, it is easy to show that each of these principles presupposes and implies the two others. Liberty, which is collective and groupal as well as individual, presupposes the equivalence of autonomous groups and free people in a fraternal union in which they are integrated and which itself freely manifests its creative spontaneity. Equality is not identity but equivalence between dissimilar individuals and groups, as well as

[1] In modern sociology, the descriptive study of pluralism *de fait* is concerned with the 'sociology of groups and forms of sociability' (which I suggested calling 'microsociology' and 'differential sociology'). Cf. my work in this area in G. Gurvitch, *Essais de sociologie*, Paris, 1938, pp. 1–112, and in *Eléments de sociologie juridique*, Paris, 1940, pp. 6–602.

equivalence between the whole and the parts; equality is therefore the very constitutive principle of an immanent, fraternal
ensemble, of a union based on collaboration, union in a 'We'
which is not alienated in a transcendent totality, and which is
not projected as an external object or superior subject outside the
multiplicity of its members, from whom it would then be separated as if by a chasm. What could the fraternity of groups and
individuals be other than a totality immanent in the plurality of
its members asserting that they are free and equal? The democratic principle is therefore in all aspects inseparable from the
pluralist ideal.

  The notion of social law. Social law, like all law, being founded
on a relationship and an interpenetration between claims and
duties,[2] is not only an order of objective law, but also a system
of 'subjective laws' to use the jurists' expression). It does not
only regulate, but attributes powers, claims, and autonomous,
creative juridical actions to interested groups and individuals.
The declarations of subjective social rights must, in the first
place, deal with these subjective social rights of groups, ensembles and individuals.

  Given that the social law is a law of integration, the social
rights proclaimed by declaration must be the *rights of participation of groups and individuals derived from their integration
in ensembles, and guaranteeing the democratic nature of these
ensembles*; the rights of the producer, the consumer and man in
general to participate in the national community, and to col-
laborate in it on an equal footing with the citizen; the right to
exercise a control over all power however it may arise in a
group or an ensemble in which the interested party is integrated;
rights of all participants to appeal to a group or an ensemble
against another group or ensemble, when their liberty appears
threatened; the right to freedom of groups, within groups
and between groups.

---

[2] The 'imperative-attributive' structure of law, according to Léon Petra-
sitzky's expression.

To complete the declaration of political rights with a declaration of social rights is to proclaim the rights of producers, consumers and men as individuals and as groups, in an effective participation in all aspects of life, work, security, welfare, education, cultural creation, as well as in all possible manifestation of juridical autonomy, democratic control by the interested parties themselves, self-government and judicial action. It is to proclaim juridically the opposite of exploitation, domination, arbitrariness, inequality, unjustified limitation of the freedom of groups and individuals wherever it is a matter of integration and participation in ensembles. Lastly, it is to proclaim the right of individuals, groups and their ensembles to a pluralist organization of society, which alone is capable of guaranteeing human freedom in contemporary conditions.

Extract from *La déclaration des droits sociaux*, New York, 1944; Paris, Vrin, 1946.

2. REJECTION OF TECHNO-BUREAUCRACY

This type of global society acquired greatest prominence in the U.S.A., in Germany before Nazism (and after it in West Germany), and also in France in recent years, particularly under the Fifth Republic. Likewise, Great Britain, Italy, and other European countries are proceeding in the same direction. In the Far East the same structure has been established in Japan, partly under the pressure of the United States.

The economy is no longer left to free competition but is planned both by the State itself—in the interest of the reigning industrial and financial upper middle class—and by private trusts and cartels (national and international), often with the support of the State, which puts its vast bureaucratic administrative machinery at their service.

Let us try to summarize briefly the structure of this global society.

(A) The State, and the trusts and cartels, whether they work together or separately, in their capacity as planning agencies serving the interests of the upper middle class, predominate over all other groups, which they seek to undermine. Political parties, the free play of constitutional institutions, democratic and civil liberties, are all dangerously compromised. The whole of political and economic life is dominated and perverted by directed capitalism. In the United States the worker's trades unions are often demoralized, if not undermined from the inside, by their adversaries. Organized capitalism will go to any lengths to break any collectivity or force which is not entirely subject to it. This is particularly easy in countries where the press, radio, television, and most universities and research institutes are dominated by private interests.

Roosevelt's New Deal represented a desperate attempt, with the help of an unprecedented crisis, to wrest economic planning from the hands of trusts and cartels by committing it to tripartite agencies—State, employers, and trades unions (freed from direct or indirect employer interference). But this experiment failed.

(B) From the microsocial point of view passive masses predominate in organized, directed capitalism. They limit active communities to public or private planning agencies, and passive communities to local groups.

(C) Organizations for economic domination and planning (utilizing automation and electronic machines) occupy first place among the depth levels. Next comes the army, whose leadership is made supremely powerful by the possession of nuclear bombs, intercontinental and interplanetary rockets, and the secret information for their operation. Workers' organizations, even when they succeed in remaining independent at the cost of constant struggle and effort (as in France and England), cannot avoid intense bureaucratization of their managerial élites. The technological patterns, as well as advertising and political slogans, are diffused by steadily improving techniques, which create a tendency towards uniformity of manufactured goods, and especially consumer goods. (In this field the U.S.A. is unsurpassed.)

(D) The onset of automation slows down the technical division of labour, and consequently also the social division of labour.

(E) We shall discuss further how technical knowledge takes the lead both in the cognitive system and in the hierarchy of social regulation, when we consider education, leisure activities, morality, and law.

(F) Technicization affects not only all kinds of knowledge and social regulation, but also 'human relations' in all their diversity. Americans consider themselves to be great experts in this field by virtue of having created a specialized occupation devoted to it.

We might briefly recall that it was in the United States that the famous doctrine of the 'managerial Society' arose, from which a new régime emerged—a 'technocracy', whose structure and cognitive system we shall analyse later. James Burnham, apart from the example of fascist societies (which he tried to make acceptable to the average American), drew mainly on the study by Berle and Means, *The Modern Corporation and Private Property* (1933), which suggested that 65 per cent of the stocks of the largest American industrial companies were divided among their managers, who thus formed a new ruling class. These findings have subsequently been disputed by numerous researchers. They have demonstrated that the data on which these conclusions were based related to only a single, short-lived economic situation, because some years later a new concentration of the stocks of these industrial companies were in the hands of large banks, which could impose their will on the managers.

Moreover, in a more recent work entitled *The Twentieth Century Capitalist Revolution* (1954), Berle himself states that the crucial element is not the transfer of stocks into the hands of the managers of trusts, but the fact that the corporate power of trusts and cartels in the United States is as strong as, if not stronger than, that of the State. The trusts and cartels account for approximately 65 per cent of all industrial ownership in the United States, and plan the economy with the national and international politics of the State.

It is not their very debatable statement that this structure is 'ineluctable' that explains our interest in Burnham and other theorists (the so-called 'liberals' of technocracy), but their implicit suggestion that managerial capitalism leads to a variously interpreted techno-bureaucratic fascism, without necessarily desiring it or knowing it. Apparently this is the only way it can maintain itself and provide a defence against the increasingly powerful threats to its existence. In fact, the essential point is that without the elimination of capitalism, democracy cannot survive.

Certainly, organized capitalism strives to conceal its intention. In the United States it works hard at improving working conditions in the factories, by combating noise and poor ventilation, remedying the discomfort of harsh lighting, and creating homogeneous work teams. Soon all workers will be working to the sound of music, with the two-fold aim of giving them satisfaction and increasing their productivity to the maximum.[3]

In France, under the Fifth Republic, triumphant directed capitalism and its techno-bureaucrats hoped to conceal the fascist tendencies of an increasingly authoritarian régime by the theatricals of a referendum and direct election of an all-powerful

[3] Another means of pacification, this time directed at the middle classes, is the development of higher education and campuses (Cités Universitaires) during the last two decades. There are approximately 3,800,000 students and 2,000 universities across the country. The author from whom we took these figures predicts 7 million students in 1970, and a proportionate increase in faculty (cf. Jacques Lusseyran, 'L'Etudiant americain', in *Esprit* (April, 1965), pp. 646–7). Although viewing this favourably, this author does not omit to point out that the universities, called 'colleges', are at a level corresponding to the highest classes in the grammar schools (*lycées*) in France, and that the higher education in the graduate schools corresponds to what until recently was called the *propédeutique* (the preparatory first year at a French university—Translator).

president. Another disguised feature is the so-called independent foreign policy, which is in fact profitable exclusively to the industrial and financial upper-middle classes, and especially to the national and international trusts and cartels. Also discussed is 'the workers' share in the profits of the enterprise', which in fact is never really accomplished under a capitalist régime, and arises from what is in fact a process of mystification.

All these façades simply bear witness to the incapacity of the ruling classes and their representatives to discern the dangers that organized capitalism presents to humanity—the enslavement of men and groups to machines, the destruction of social structures and cultural works by increasingly autonomous techniques, progressive denial of workers' rights and those of their organizations, and, more generally, of the rights of all citizens (producers and consumers) to govern themselves and to control whatever power seeks to impose itself on them. The authoritarianism of the 'sorcerer's apprentices', whether they be political rulers, employers, their trusts and cartels, or the technocrats in their service, is increasingly acknowledged. And yet the explosive forces that it unleashed go uncontrolled. Thus organized and directed capitalism moves steadily towards the type of structure and society characteristic of technocratic fascism.

Extract from 'Les cadres sociaux de la connaissance', Paris, Presses Universtitaires de France, 1966. English translation 'The social frameworks of knowledge' by M. A. and K. A. Thompson, Basil Blackwell, Oxford, 1971.

BIBLIOGRAPHY

Balandier, G. 'Georges Gurvitch', in *Cah. int. Socio.*, XL, 1966.
Balandier, G. (*et al*). *Perspectives de la sociologie contemporaine, hommage à Georges Gurvitch*, Paris, 1968.
Bosserman, P. *Dialectical Sociology, an analysis of the sociology of Georges Gurvitch*, Boston, 1968.
Braudel, F. 'Georges Gurvitch ou la discontinuité du social', in *Annales*, July-Sept., 1953.
Cazeneuve, J. 'La sociologie de Georges Gurvitch', in *Rev. franç. Socio.*, II, 1, January-March 1966.
Dourado, M. *O Fato normativo e a Objectividade do Direito*, Rio de Janeiro, 1933.
Duvignaud, J. *Georges Gurvitch, symbolisme social et sociologie dynamique*, Paris, 1969.
Gits, C. *Recht, Persoon en Gemeenschap*, Louvain, 1949.
Sorokin, P. *Sociological Theories of Today*, New York, 1966.
Tiryakian, E. *Sociologism and Existentialism*, Englewood Cliffs, 1962.
Toulemont, R. *Sociologie et pluralisme dialectique, introduction à l'oeuvre de Georges Gurvitch*, Louvain-Paris, 1955.
Wiese, L. V. 'Gurvitch's Beruf der Soziologie', in *Kölner Zeitschrift für Soziologie*, 2–3, 4er Jahrgang 1951–2.